FATHER
OF
SKYSCRAPERS

A Biography of Louis Sullivan

Louis was forty-four when this picture was taken in 1900.

FATHER
OF
SKYSCRAPERS

A Biography of Louis Sullivan

by

MERVYN KAUFMAN

ILLUSTRATED WITH PHOTOGRAPHS

BOSTON   LITTLE, BROWN AND COMPANY   TORONTO

Published simultaneously in Canada
by Little, Brown & Company (Canada) Limited

PRINTED IN THE UNITED STATES OF AMERICA

For Nancy, with whom everything
has become possible.

CONTENTS

	List of Illustrations	ix
I	A Country Boyhood	3
II	Boston	17
III	A Year at Tech	30
IV	To the West	43
V	Mr. Adler	56
VI	The Great Auditorium	73
VII	Buildings That Soar	94
VIII	The Golden Doorway	113
IX	The Years with Margaret	128
X	Louis Alone	142
	Glossary	161
	Acknowledgments	165
	Index	167

LIST OF ILLUSTRATIONS

Louis Sullivan at age forty-four	*Frontispiece*
Henri List, Louis's grandfather	4
Andrienne Sullivan, Louis's mother	5
Patrick Sullivan, Louis's father	5
Albert and Louis Sullivan as youngsters	5
A New England farmhouse of the 1860's	6
Washington Street, Boston, late 1860's	19
Massachusetts State House, Boston	20
Residences in Louisburg Square, Boston	21
Louis Sullivan at fourteen	27
M.I.T. when Louis was a student	37
The architect Henry Hobson Richardson	40
Richardson's Brattle Square Church, Boston	40
Furness's Provident Life and Trust Building	47
Furness's Guarantee Trust Building, Philadelphia	47
Clark Street, Chicago, about 1868	52
La Salle Street, Chicago, before the fire	52
Ruins of Chicago, after the great fire, 1871	53
Detail of Richardson's Trinity Church, Boston	65
Full view of Trinity Church	65
Louis Sullivan at twenty	66
Sullivan's partner, Dankmar Adler	68
Adler & Sullivan's Borden Block, Chicago	71
Burnham & Root's Monadnock Building, Chicago	74
Major Jenney's Home Insurance Building	76
Auditorium Building: Sullivan's initial design	84
Auditorium Building: revised design	84
Auditorium Building, completed	89
Auditorium, view toward balcony and galleries	90

The Auditorium's decorative ceiling arches	91
Inside the Auditorium on night of gala reopening	91
Adler & Sullivan's Walker Warehouse, Chicago	95
Richardson's Marshall Field Wholesale Store	95
Louis Sullivan at thirty-four	97
Louis's cottage at Ocean Springs, Mississippi	99
The home built for Louis's mother, Chicago	100
Wainwright Building, St. Louis, full view	104
Wainwright Building, exterior detail	104
Schiller Building, Chicago	106
Louis at the piano, sketched by his mother	108
Louis's brother, Albert Sullivan	110
Mary Spelman, who became Albert's wife	111
The architect Daniel Burnham	114
Burnham's partner, John Root	115
World's Fair, Chicago, 1893: Court of Honor	117
View of Chicago Fair from Main Basin	117
Transportation Building, Chicago Fair	118
Golden Doorway, Transportation Building	120
Guaranty (now Prudential) Building, Buffalo	122
Guaranty Building, foyer	123
Guaranty Building, stairs and elevator cages	123
Bayard Building, New York City	130
Exterior ornament: Carson, Pirie, Scott store	133
Carson, Pirie, Scott & Company, Chicago	134
Louis and his wife Margaret at Ocean Springs	138
National Farmers' Bank, Owatonna, Minnesota	144
National Farmers' Bank, tellers' cages	145
National Farmers' Bank, interior doorway	145
The architect Frank Lloyd Wright	147
Evans House, Chicago, designed by Wright	148
Wright's Larkin Building, Buffalo, interior	148
The last portrait made of Sullivan, 1920	150
Krause Music Store, Sullivan's last work	151
A drawing from Sullivan's book on ornament	154
One of the drawings Sullivan gave to Wright	157

FATHER
OF
SKYSCRAPERS

A Biography of Louis Sullivan

I

A COUNTRY BOYHOOD

THE WINDING DIRT ROAD that linked outlying farms to the Massachusetts town of South Reading was normally quiet. Only the tinkling cry of a bobolink could be heard, or the sound of wagon wheels grinding in the roadway's hardened ruts. Otherwise there was silence. But on an autumn morning in the early 1860's the road to South Reading fairly rang with noise.

A small boy, round-faced and red with anger, was being led by his grandparents — or dragged, it seemed — to his first day at a new school. A slightly older boy was with them, trying to ignore the commotion. He walked along briskly, eager to reach the classroom, but it was clear that the younger boy, his brother, shared none of his enthusiasm.

"No, no, *no!*" the little boy cried again and again, each time kicking defiantly and trying to wrench himself free. His grandparents were obviously upset, but they kept a tight hold on him.

"There, there, child, you'll make yourself ill," said his grandmother, hoping to calm him.

"It won't be so bad once you get there," his grandfather said reassuringly. "There's nothing to worry about, you'll see." But the boy refused to be pacified. His shouts and shrieks of protest continued to split the air. It was not that Louis Sullivan feared the unfamiliarity of a new school. It was simply that he could not face meeting new classmates the way he was dressed. His grandmother had spent long evenings sewing and stitching by dim candlelight, so Louis would have something special to wear on that important first day. She loved her grandsons equally, but as Louis was the younger one, she usually went out of her way to please him first.

But this time he was not pleased at all. The moment he put on the floppy black bow tie and the little white jacket, *and* the white pantalets that were gathered in delicate ruffles at the ankles, he knew he was going to be unhappy. Then when his grandfather placed a large straw hat on Louis's head and anchored it with a ribbon strung beneath his chin, the boy nearly exploded. Sputtering and gasping through spasms of tears, he declared he could *not* go to school in such clothes. He would not have other children jeering at him.

"But think of all the trouble I went to," his grandmother pleaded. "Now, your grandpa and I will go there with you, so you needn't be afraid." They each took him by a hand and led him down the road toward the schoolhouse, but they did not get very far. As they dearly loved the little boy, they found his painful,

Henri List, Louis's grandfather

Andrienne Sullivan, Louis's mother

Patrick Sullivan, his father

Louis (right) and his older brother Albert

The New England farmhouses Louis knew as a boy were little changed from those of colonial times. Farmhouse design was basic; mills, schools and meetinghouses were derived from it.

anguished sobbing unbearable. Their shingle-covered farmhouse was still in sight when they finally turned and headed back.

The straw hat, the bow tie, the jacket and the pantalets were tucked into a cedar chest. Louis Sullivan had fought and won the first big battle of his life. He would never be less obstinate or less determined in anything he did.

He had been born in Boston on September 3, 1856, two years after his brother Albert. His father, Patrick Sullivan, was a ballroom-dancing teacher. While Louis and Albert were youngsters, the Sullivans traveled widely throughout New England, as Patrick opened — and closed — one dancing school after another. When business in a town dropped off the family moved to another, and in the summer they followed their wealthier clientele to the seashore. They rarely stayed in one place very long.

By the time the boys were both in school, their mother, Andrienne Sullivan, had begun to worry that the frequent moves would hamper their education. Her parents suggested that the boys come to live with them. Their twenty-four-acre farm in South

Reading was ten miles north of Boston. Andrienne refused at first, not wanting to be separated from her sons, but Patrick finally persuaded her to let the boys live awhile with their grandparents. Patrick was fond of Louis and Albert, but he knew that, freed from the responsibility of looking after them, Andrienne would have more time to help him with his classes, playing the piano and taking care of some of the youngsters who were his pupils.

So the Sullivan boys went to live with their Grandpa and Grandma List, who were overjoyed at the prospect. Having children in their midst again would brighten their lives as nothing else could. The day before the boys arrived, Grandma List had rushed to finish the suit of clothes she planned for Louis to wear to school. She was disappointed, of course, by the way he reacted to them, but her disappointment was not as keen as her desire to make Louis happy. Later she laid out the suit his mother had made. It was a plain tweed with knee breeches and long hose, just like the one that Albert wore. The next day the boys and their grandparents set out once more on the road to the schoolhouse, and this time they went all the way.

Like many of the farmhouses in New England, the South Reading school was a white clapboard structure with dark shutters and a high sloping roof. It was set on a hillside just outside the town. The students who went there, girls as well as boys, were mostly from farms nearby, plainly dressed, some of them barefoot. Louis thought of the outfit his grandmother had sewn and was glad he had made such a fuss. He certainly would have felt out of place wearing it.

Louis and his brother were assigned to a large classroom in which five grades were taught at once. Each grade occupied a single row of desks that faced, one behind another, toward the teacher at the front of the room. She sat on a raised platform and held a small rattan switch in her hand, ready to reward a student's inattentiveness or misbehavior with a stinging rap on the palm.

A row of desks separated Louis from Albert, for the boys were two grades apart. Being a timid newcomer, Louis talked to no one but silently observed his classmates, and pondered a classroom routine that never seemed to vary. Pupils worked at the lessons until their particular grade was summoned to recite. They would then line up at the front of the room, their backs to the wall, to be questioned one by one. Depending on how each of them answered, the teacher would say, "Go to the head of the class," or "Go to the foot." The students tended to mumble their replies, so Louis could not hear them well from where he sat. But he was aware of their shifting about — to the head of the class and to the foot.

Albert was a good, hard-working student who found himself at the head of the class fairly often. But Louis's customary place was at the foot — not because the work was hard, but because it clearly bored him. He was more interested in what the older pupils were being taught, finding little to challenge him in the assignments he was given.

Perturbed by Louis's indifference, the teacher wrote his grandparents a letter, which Grandpa List read aloud at the supper table. Louis, the teacher reported, was a nice boy but a dull student, sad to say. He did not pay attention; he would not prepare his lessons; he was always at the foot of his class.

Grandpa List reacted by laughing out loud. Louis Sullivan dull? How ridiculous! "There isn't a thing on earth this child doesn't want to know," he exclaimed, patting Louis affectionately on the head. Grandpa dropped the letter and laughed again, but Grandma was not amused. She made Louis stand tall, and she lectured him sternly. It was important that he mend his ways, she said, for he could not expect to get ahead in the world without an education. "You're just as smart as your brother," she declared. "You belong at the *head* of the class, not the foot." Louis kissed her repeatedly, for he knew displays of affection would keep him from being punished. But he promised to try to improve his record.

It was not hard for him to go to the head of his class, or to stay there, either. When he prepared his lessons he could answer any question the teacher asked, and when he tried he could recite better than all the other students. In no time his record changed completely.

Cheered by his progress, the teacher kept up a barrage of encouragement. Her praise was boundless . . . but he could not keep up the good work. When spring arrived, his restlessness returned. He was a child of nature and the out-of-doors drew him to it like a firm, beckoning hand.

"If I didn't go to school, would that be bad?" Louis asked his brother one day as they were walking home.

"That would be playing hooky," said Albert. "Teacher wouldn't like it."

"She'd tell Grandpa and Grandma, wouldn't she?" Louis asked.

"Probably," said Albert.

"Would *you*?" Louis asked.

Albert thought a moment and then, aware of his brother's intent expression, said, "No, I wouldn't tell, I guess. And if teacher asks, I'll say you're sick. O.K.?" Louis nodded and said nothing more the rest of the way home.

Several days later, quite early in the morning, Louis tiptoed into the kitchen and stuffed a generous supply of doughnuts, rolls and cookies inside his shirt. He had his books under his arm as he headed down the road, but once out of sight of the List farmhouse he turned and ran off to the fields. He was bound for a stream he had seen once on a walk with his grandfather. He was going to build a dam!

Following a path to a wooded ravine, he came to a shady spot where the stream flowed swiftly beneath an arch of trees. It was there, he had decided, his dam should be built.

He had watched hired men gather stones to erect farm walls. Now he did as they had done, collecting fieldstones as big as he could carry. He found a rusty hoe without a handle and used it to dig up chunks of earth. Then he laid the stones row upon row, and between each stone he placed mud, twigs and grass to hold the rows together.

The higher the water rose in the dam, the faster and harder Louis worked. He had to keep raising the dam to hold the water back. At the same time he had to patch the leaks that sprang here and there, where water pressure overcame his construction. Finally the leaking stopped; the sound of trickling water faded away; the dam was finished.

He stood back and looked at it a moment, thrilled at having fashioned a barrier sturdy enough to halt the stream. Then with all his strength he applied the hoe to the center of the wall and tore it open. The trapped water gushed through the break, and Louis shouted with glee. The dam was a wreck, but that had been his purpose. He had proved he had the skill to build it — and the power to destroy it as well. Nothing at school could compare with what he had done.

For the next month Louis spent his school days out of doors. He carried food, mostly sweets, inside his shirt and brought a tin cup with him so he could milk an obliging cow if he became thirsty. He explored the countryside, spending day after day tramping across the wide swath of meadow, hillock and ravine that he considered his domain.

Louis did not spend all his time away from school in solitude. Often he talked to farmers planting corn, to shoemakers pounding leather, or to men molding iron in a stove foundry. All of them seemed to enjoy his company, for he was an amusing little boy — plump, freckled from the sun and toothless from the process of growing. His breeches were rolled above his knees and a thatch of black hair fell in unruly clumps about his forehead. He seemed a ragamuffin, a free spirit roaming unrestrained. Surely there could not have been a happier truant . . . but neither his freedom nor his truancy would last.

One day another letter came to Grandpa List from Louis's teacher. This one reported that Louis had been absent from school a full month. Little was said at home, but Louis could see that his grandparents were disturbed. Even though he returned to the classroom, as he had known he would have to eventually, Grandma List wrote his mother to report what he had done.

The Sullivans knew right away what the problem was. Their younger son needed discipline, the kind of strong guidance two loving and lenient grandparents could not give. There was no question about it: the time had come for Louis to return to his mother and father. When school was out for the summer, Andrienne prepared to go to South Reading, and Louis began packing his things.

He would miss the farm, the fields, his brother and his grandparents, of course, but he welcomed the idea of being back with his parents. And he looked forward to the train trip he would take with his mother. Together they were to go to Newburyport, on the coast of northern Massachusetts, where his father had opened a dancing school for the summer.

Rail travel was an ordeal in the 1860's. Passenger cars were stuffy and hot, and the closed windows kept out little of the dust and grime that accumulated along the way. The rattling, jolting, bumping motions of the train, combined with its noisy clanking and screeching, made riding comfort impossible.

To Andrienne Sullivan the prospect of making a train trip was never a pleasant one. She was a pale, fragile-looking woman who trembled at the howl of a locomotive's whistle and started at the hiss of its brakes. The confusion at the station, the jostling of people as they moved to and fro, wore her out. After helping Louis aboard the train, she steered him to a pair of seats in an uncrowded car and settled wearily into the worn, faded cushions.

Louis, by contrast, was bubbling with anticipation. He peered through the window and bounced in his seat as the train pulled out of the station. In no time he was asking a steady stream of questions: "Why do the trees go by so fast . . . why do the telegraph wires rise and fall?" His queries flowed without stopping, hardly giving his mother a chance to answer. Soon she was only nodding, saying nothing. Her eyes closed finally, and she fell fast asleep.

Louis looked around for someone else to talk to, but the other passengers were also dozing, so he wandered restlessly up and down the aisle. Finally he slid open the door of the car, determined to explore the train's entire length. He stood on the shallow platform between his car and the next one, gazing down at the rails speeding by beneath him. The flashing of shiny steel and the rhythmic jouncing of the cars were almost hypnotic. In a moment he was lost in thought and almost lost for good, for the train swung sharply as it rounded a curve, and Louis was flung off balance.

As he began to fall, he reached out for something to cling to but found nothing there. An instant before panic seized him, he felt himself being grabbed about the waist and lifted to his feet by a pair of thick, strong arms. When he had caught his breath, he turned and faced a man in overalls whose dry, leathery skin told of a long life in the out-of-doors.

The man was furious. He swore at Louis, demanding to know why the boy had come out on the platform, where it was so dangerous to be. Not intimidated easily, Louis answered by asking some questions of his own: "What does 'telegraph' mean, mister? And what makes those clicking noises under the train?" The man was taken aback by the little boy's boldness. When his anger had cooled he was able to answer most of Louis's questions. In no time Louis had made a friend of his rescuer, who turned out to be one of the brakemen.

The next time the train stopped, the brakeman took Louis off and showed him how the cars were coupled together and the way the wheels were braked. Louis wanted to go forward and ask the engineer and fireman their names, but the brakeman, whose name Louis never knew, hauled him abruptly back aboard. The train started up, and Louis returned to his seat.

He woke his mother now, for he was bursting with the news of having met a fascinating man who had befriended him. Andrienne merely smiled and patted his hand, urging him to remain at her side for the rest of the trip. After he was certain he had told her everything, he curled his feet under him and leaned against her shoulder. The train, rumbling and swaying along its route, rocked him to sleep. The next thing Louis knew, the brake wheels were grinding, and the train was losing speed. Then the conductor's voice called out, "Newburyport . . . Newburyport." The Sullivans, mother and son, were home.

Their home that summer was an old hotel that stood across the square from the Newburyport town hall. It was a Gothic structure, narrow, with high ceilings and windows the shape of pointed arches. Even to Louis's unschooled eyes the hotel seemed a gloomy place. It was run-down from years of neglect, and the people who stayed there were not vacationers on holiday but transients like Louis's mother and father.

None of them were particularly friendly. At mealtime they all gathered in the dining room and sat down at a long, drab table. Normally no one spoke, except to ask in a whisper that a platter be passed. But Louis broke this silence at his very first meal. In a voice loud enough to be heard in the pantry, he announced that the gravy being served was not as good as his grandmother made. In fact, he said, it was hardly more than flour mixed with water.

His mother blushed and clenched his arm, hardly daring to look up from her plate. None of the other diners looked up either, but some of them tittered. Though they all knew the gravy was tasteless, none of them would have said so. It had been left to a child to give voice to their feelings.

Later, despite the rightness of his judgment, Louis was taken aside and given his first lesson in etiquette. His mother admonished him to speak only when spoken to, to speak softly even then and say, "Yes, sir," "No, sir," "Yes, ma'am" and "No, ma'am" to his elders. Louis's father, a wiry, dark-haired man, firm of limb and generally gruff in nature, had no use for such formalities. It made no difference to him whether Louis learned manners. He cared only that his sons grow up healthy and strong. At 5 A.M. the morning after Louis had arrived, Patrick awakened him with loud, insistent handclaps.

"Time to get up, son," he called out. "We arise bright and early in Newburyport." Without waiting for Louis to respond, Patrick removed the bedding and pulled the startled boy to his feet. After Louis had climbed sleepily into some clothes, his father said, "Follow me," and the two of them went outside, crossing the square to the water pump, which stood before the town hall. Patrick gave the pump handle a few swift strokes, allowing enough water to splash on his arm so he could test the temperature. Then he filled a cup and handed it to Louis. "Drink it down," he commanded, "all at once."

Louis took a deep breath and put the cup to his lips. "Is it cold enough?" his father asked, and the boy replied with a shudder. The water was colder than any he had ever tasted. He took a few sips, and when he stopped drinking he was gasping for breath.

"If you feel chilly, we'll have to run now," his father said. "It's good for the circulation." Patrick finished the cup of water himself and set off at a trot. After a few blocks, he slowed down so Louis could catch up. "Let's walk awhile," said Patrick, but he continued to set a brisk pace. The two of them covered two full miles in a very short time. They stopped, finally, when they came to a pool of water fed by the sea.

"Off with your clothes," Patrick cried. And though the sharp morning air made him shiver, Louis removed his clothing just as his father did. Then Patrick picked him up and tossed him into the water. Down he went, into an icy wetness that almost numbed him, and up he came, sputtering and choking up mouthfuls of water. By this time Patrick had dived in beside him. Treading water, he placed a strong arm under Louis's chest and began teaching the boy to swim.

"We mustn't stay in long. It's kind of cold," said Patrick after

a few moments. "Want to *ride* back to shore, son?" Louis replied
that he did — very much! — and clambered eagerly onto his father's back. He clung to Patrick's hair as his father swam toward
dry land.

Each morning from then on Louis and his father drank cold
water from the pump, ran together to improve their wind, walked
swiftly to stimulate their blood and swam naked in the saltwater
pool. In addition to the daily exercise there were also outings for
all three Sullivans that summer, one of which was a Sunday
picnic beside the Merrimack River. As Andrienne unfolded a
bright checkered cloth and laid out the food, Louis watched huge
sturgeon leap out of the water, leaving wide ripples as they then
fell back beneath the surface.

Louis observed the fish with fascination, for they were bigger
than the minnows and sunfish he had known in South Reading.
The river, too, was a larger body of water than he had ever seen.
After lunch, while his parents were resting, he walked along the
curving riverbank and poked his way into a grove of trees. The
underbrush was thick, so he had to step carefully. The trees grew
so close together that their limbs intertwined, shutting out sunlight and forcing Louis to feel his way through deep shadows.
Beyond the limbs and tree trunks he could still see the water
glistening in the sun, for as he moved along, his path was running parallel to the river's flow.

Suddenly he stopped, frozen in fright. Through the trees a huge
dark object loomed ominously ahead, a thing so enormous that it
stretched from one riverbank to the other. Louis saw what looked
like two stone giants from whose arms chains dangled as though
floating in midair. He was certain the object was coming toward
him and stood transfixed — unable to move — in mortal fear of
being eaten alive or trampled to death.

A loud cracking of leaves and twigs distracted him, and he
cried out. The sounds came nearer, and suddenly Louis saw his
father peering at him through the shadows. Patrick had come

looking for the boy, intending to reward Louis's wandering off with a spanking. But one look at Louis's terrified expression changed his manner.

"What's the matter, son?" Patrick cried, and Louis threw himself on his father, blurting out a stream of incoherencies. Patrick patted the boy gently to calm him. Then, taking his hand, he led Louis out of the woods, explaining as he went that the large object was not a giant but a new suspension bridge that spanned the river. The chains Louis had seen held up a roadway. The stone giants were really structural towers at either end of the bridge.

When his fear had subsided, Louis walked across the bridge with his father. He crossed it twice, marveling at the fortresslike strength of its stonework and the thickness of its supporting chains. He could scarcely believe it had been built by men. How fearless they must have been, defying the winds and the river's dizzying current to raise the mighty towers and hoist the suspension rigging. And to think that horses and wagons filled to overflowing could be led across the bridge with no fear of its collapsing!

Later that summer Patrick took Louis to a shipyard, where he was held in thrall by the fast-paced symphony of men working with hand tools — wedges, adzes and mallets. Nothing seemed as exciting now as what men had the power to make, and the bigger a structure the more exhilarated Louis became.

He had grown to love Newburyport, for during his short stay he had gone places and observed things he had never seen before. But at summer's end Patrick closed his dancing school. Andrienne packed the family's belongings, and the Sullivans left the bleak hotel. They boarded a train for Boston, where they planned to stay all winter, and where, ultimately, a new kind of life awaited Louis.

II

BOSTON

TO A BOY who had spent most of his life in small towns or on a farm, Boston seemed a strange, forbidding place. In the heart of the city Louis saw houses and buildings of all sizes standing as close together as hogs at a trough. Streets were narrow and crooked. Animal odors and the stench of garbage choked the air. Dense crowds of people rushed about on foot, and wagons full of goods and produce rumbled noisily over the cobblestone pavements.

From his first day in Boston Louis found himself wistfully recalling South Reading. There was nothing in the city — not the sights, the sounds or the smells — that appealed to him. Certainly his relief was great when he learned that his first exposure to Boston would be brief. For Patrick had experienced a change of heart about working there. He suddenly decided that his prospects might be better farther north, in Halifax, Nova Scotia. Louis and his mother had no sooner unpacked when Patrick ordered them to quickly pack again. They piled their bags aboard a train bound for Eastport, Maine, and there booked passage on a boat that sailed the choppy waters of the Bay of Fundy, skirting the Nova Scotia coast.

What followed for Louis was a cold and terrible winter, for Patrick remained as determined as ever to turn his chubby little boy into a strapping young man. In freezing temperatures, as often as the extremes of weather permitted, the two of them walked for many miles, their heads bowed to piercing winds. At the end of these treks, when Louis was exhausted, he was made to follow his father's example and bathe his face in snow. Patrick said the snow was invigorating, but Louis shivered and pinched his own cheeks to check their numbness. His only happy memory of the months in Nova Scotia was of watching men at work blasting a deep trench into which water pipes were laid. Bundled in thick, fur-lined clothing, they hacked their way into a ledge of solid slate. Louis watched until the sharp cold air made his eyes water. He never ceased to marvel at the things men could do.

When the northern winter was coldest, Andrienne Sullivan became ill with diphtheria. For weeks she lay in bed, weak and feverish. When spring came, the fever gradually subsided, but Patrick's concern for her persisted. He decided they would have to return to Boston. At that point, assuredly, anyplace would have seemed better to Louis than Halifax. In no time he had almost forgotten he had ever been there. Albert rejoined the family in Boston, and for the next several years both boys stayed with their parents in wintertime and spent summers with their grandparents on the farm.

In 1868, the summer Louis was twelve and Albert fourteen, South Reading received a new name. Cyrus Wakefield, a wealthy businessman, offered to finance the building of a new town hall if in exchange the town were renamed after him. The people who lived there accepted this proposal, and South Reading, which Louis Sullivan always considered his childhood home, became a place called Wakefield.

As he grew older Louis began to take the town for granted, and as his knowledge of Boston increased the city began to fascinate him. Albert was too much absorbed in his studies to care about Boston, for the courses at the elite Latin School were difficult. But since schoolwork was hardly more than drudgery for Louis, he gave it as little attention as he had to. His father had enrolled him in the Brimmer School, which Louis considered a prison for children. He did not play hooky as he once did, but he could hardly wait for school to end each day so he could brighten his spirits by

Washington Street in downtown Boston was usually bustling and busy. But to take this picture in the 1860's, long before fast lenses, the street had to be cleared of movement.

This is how the Massachusetts State House looked when Louis was exploring Boston. Later, wings were added to either side of the building, and the dome was covered in bright gold leaf.

visiting some corner of the city he had never seen. His mother insisted that he learn to play the piano, but he quit his lessons after a time because he preferred being outdoors to practicing.

He walked the length and breadth of Boston, from the teeming docks with their pungent fish smells to the peak of Beacon Hill, where the domed State House stood. Soon he realized how much more there was to the city than the clanking of wagons and the sharp cries of peddlers hawking their wares. He found excitement in what had merely seemed hubbub. He also found history, for Boston was as much a city of tradition as it was of growth.

Downtown in the market district there was Faneuil Hall, where patriots had gathered secretly in Revolutionary times. Nearby was the Old North Church, from whose tower a lantern had been hung as a signal from Paul Revere that British troops were marching on Lexington and Concord. And Louis never wearied of looking at majestic Park Street Church, built on what was once called Brimstone Corner. In a granary where the church now stands, gunpowder was stored during the War of 1812 and the sails of heroic "Old Ironsides," the fighting frigate *Constitution,* were made.

Louis could trace the growth of the city as he scoured its streets and alleys. He could see that the wooden structures were the oldest — some dating from Colonial times. Their simplicity of design contributed to their beauty, though many of them were in disuse, their front stoops sagging from age. The buildings erected in the early nineteenth century were generally larger and more formal, their walls made of red brick laid in straight courses. Louis found the handsomest of these structures in the residential areas where prosperous Bostonians lived. There, along wide

Among Boston's finest homes are those that stand along the perimeter of Louisburg Square. These well-maintained dwellings have been modified only slightly since the 19th century.

streets lined with elm or linden trees, he saw fine mansions surrounded by gardens and well-kept stables.

Some of Boston's most recent buildings were made of granite, dark gray stones hauled from quarries that had been opened some miles inland from the city a generation before Louis's birth. Walking about Boston, Louis not only observed differences in the shapes and outer surfaces of buildings, but from careful study he also discovered that the basic structure of buildings was being changed.

In many of the new office buildings the beams, balconies, railings, window frames — sometimes even the facades — were being made of cast iron. Previously, metal had been used for construction only in bridge-building. Its new application reflected great progress in engineering and pointed the way toward a revolution in building design that Louis himself would be part of one day.

Louis always enjoyed watching the construction process. He was stirred by the sight of muscular workmen bolting granite blocks into place. He marveled at sculptors perched on spindly scaffolds, chiseling scrollwork into rough stone surfaces. He envied the men who could create new, exciting forms from unwieldy materials. He began to think that perhaps *he* might want to work on a construction team.

One day as he was strolling down tree-lined Commonwealth Avenue, a tall man in top hat and frock coat came out of an unfinished building and crossed the walk in front of him. The man carried himself with dignity: a proud, erect figure with the air of regal eminence. Louis watched him climb into a waiting carriage and signal his coachman to drive away. A fine horse, its coat curried to a sunlit sheen, pulled the carriage down the street.

The man was important; there could be no doubting it. It was apparent from everything about him: his coach, his clothes, his aristocratic stride. Louis was eager to know the man's identity, and since he seldom allowed his curiosity to go unsatisfied, he called out to one of the workmen, "Excuse me, sir, who was that gentleman who just went away?"

"The tall fellow? He's the architect of this building," the workman said. Louis had never heard that word before. What was an architect, he wanted to know — the owner of the building?

"Nah, he don't own the place," the workman replied sharply. "He *designed* it."

"You mean he's your boss?" Louis asked, uncomprehending.

"See that man in overalls? He's *my* boss," the workman explained, pointing toward a heavyset man with glasses. "The supervisor is *his* boss, and the architect's the boss of everybody."

"How come he's so important?" Louis asked.

"Because he thought up the plans for the building," the workman said. "He makes up buildings out of his head."

Louis was dumbfounded. He had never imagined such a thing. He had assumed that the workmen decided what kind of building they wanted and built it to look that way. It had never occurred to him that someone else was involved, a man who created every detail of a building before construction began. What a great and remarkable man an architect must be, he thought. What an imagination he must have. What power! In an instant, as he stood looking quizzically at the workman, he had made a decision. "I'm going to be an architect, too," he announced.

The man seemed dubious and scratched his chin. "I don't know about that," he said. "You've got to know a lot first. You need a good education."

"I'm still in school," Louis assured him, "and I'll go as long as I have to."

The workman was still unconvinced. "To tell the truth, I don't think you have the right kind of brains. You've got a faraway look in your eyes that makes me think maybe you won't be practical, and you've got to be practical to be an architect. Know what I mean?"

Louis nodded that he did and thanked the man, but he said his mind was made up and that was that. He did not publicize his decision, however. His brother Albert repeatedly spoke of plans to go off to sea, but Louis kept silent about his own intentions. There were times, though, when he became so lost in thought about his future that people had to speak twice before he heard them.

That year, in the summer of 1869, Louis's parents decided to move to Chicago. Patrick had no knowledge of Chicago's unpredictable weather, but he assumed the climate would be better for Andrienne's health than Boston. She had become ill with diphtheria again the previous winter, and though she had recovered, Patrick still feared for her life. Albert was to go west with his parents. Being midway through high school — and an excellent student — he could go anywhere without disrupting his studies. Louis, on the other hand, was to stay behind and live with his Grandma and Grandpa List, at least until he had finished grammar school.

Shortly before the elder Sullivans left Boston, Louis told his father what he wanted to do. Patrick seemed delighted that Louis's ambition had finally found focus. He talked at length about architecture's being a great art and a noble profession. Then he took Louis by surprise and suggested something entirely different.

"You love the out-of-doors . . . you're happy on the farm. Why not let me send you to an agricultural college instead?" said Patrick. "I have enough money saved to keep you in school at least until you're twenty-one. If you study hard, someday you can become a *scientific farmer.*" The words had a special ring because of the emphasis he gave them. He spoke with relish about blooded stock, fertilizers, soil chemistry and plant cross-fertilization. And all the while Louis's mouth was agape. He had never heard his father speak so eloquently about anything before. He couldn't understand what had made Patrick become so enthusiastic about agriculture.

When Patrick was finished, he turned to his son. "Well, does it sound like a good idea?" he asked. Louis was silent, seemingly lost in thought. If he experienced uncertainty, it never showed, for after a moment he shook his head, no. But Patrick did not give up. In the few days left, he tried more than once to motivate his son toward scientific farming.

When Louis said goodbye to his parents, he wept without shame on his mother's shoulder. Because of her delicate state of health, he did not know if he would ever see her again, but he was admittedly relieved to see his father leave Boston. Despite his resolve, he knew he could not have withstood many of Patrick's attempts to change his mind. Away from his father, however, Louis was now free to pursue his own interests.

His dislike of school was still intense, but when he transferred to the brand-new Rice Grammar School everything changed for the better. The building was attractive, with a warm, inviting atmosphere. Its newness, brightness and cleanness made him feel comfortable and at peace. And he became aware from this reaction how the design of a building could strongly affect the people who used it.

Suddenly he did not hate school any more. Because of the pleasant surroundings, he actually looked forward to going. Like a tide that mysteriously changes direction, Louis became a devoted reader of books. Many of the lessons he had once found boring now at last seemed interesting. His grammar book absorbed him. The dos and don'ts of language and the ironclad rules of speech ignited a glow of enthusiasm in him. He took to geography, too, to some extent, but his interests did not extend to history. The people described in his textbook did not seem real to him, and the stories were mostly about wars, which he did not like.

Another course he disliked was "speaking pieces." A streak of bashfulness had developed in him. He became self-conscious at the thought of standing before the class and giving a recitation. Besides, he found little of value in any of the pieces the class had to recite. He particularly despised "Old Ironsides," the poem Oliver Wendell Holmes had written in 1828 when that great ship, a veteran of naval triumphs in the War of 1812, was condemned as unseaworthy. It was an emotional poem, one that had aroused so much public sentiment at the time that the ship had been saved from destruction. "Old Ironsides" was the favorite poem of many a schoolteacher, including his own, so it should not have surprised Louis when he was asked to come to the front of the room one day and recite it.

After his name was called, he got up slowly and approached the platform. His bashfulness was gone. His hands trembled not in fear but in silent rage as he turned to face the class. He paused a moment. Then in a voice as loud as a frightened cabin boy's, he shouted the poem's opening line: *"Ay, tear her tattered ensign down!"* His classmates roared with delight, but his teacher halted the recitation and sent him back to his seat. Then she left the room.

The class was even more delighted now, stirred by fanciful visions of the kind of punishment Louis would get. When she returned a few minutes later, she said very sternly, "Louis Sullivan, you are to go see the headmaster." Everyone cheered as Louis left the room.

The headmaster, Mr. Wheelock, was a roundish fellow with bright blue eyes and a curly blond beard. His face usually wore a happy expression, but not today. The Mr. Wheelock who glared at Louis from behind a large wooden desk was sinister-looking and he held a long rattan switch. "I understand you have insulted your teacher before the class," Mr. Wheelock began. He gave the switch a couple of frightening flicks into the palm of his hand. "What have you to say for yourself?"

Louis apologized without any coaxing. He was fond of his teacher, he said, and had not intended to insult her. Mr. Wheelock raised an eyebrow and nodded, but the switch remained firmly in his grasp. Louis knew that switch could inflict painful welts on its victims, and he resolved right then that it would never touch him. He would talk as long as was necessary to avoid the punishment.

He said, first off, "The poem is claptrap." Mr. Wheelock re-

Louis Sullivan at fourteen

sponded by vibrating the arm that held the rattan. Then Louis proceeded to take the poem apart line by line and stanza by stanza, explaining what he thought was wrong with it. Mr. Wheelock's expression changed from anger to puzzlement, which convinced Louis that the headmaster was beginning to be impressed. As Louis continued to talk, Mr. Wheelock leaned back in his chair, and his eyes took on a twinkle. Finally, he put down the switch.

There was a moment's pause when Louis had finished. "That was a fine speech," said Mr. Wheelock. "When you got through with Oliver Holmes, you left his poem as tattered as his ensign." Then, chuckling, he rose from his big chair and patted Louis's shoulder. "I'm glad we had it out, lad. I might have thrashed you in anger if you hadn't spoken up. Now go back to your class. And even if you *don't* like the poems you recite . . . in the future be more considerate of a woman's feelings." Louis manfully shook the headmaster's hand and left the office.

All eyes were upon him as he reentered the room. His classmates searched his face for the red flush of pain or the telltale streaks of dried tears, but there was nothing to see. Louis mounted the platform solemnly and apologized to his teacher for the way he had behaved. Then he took his seat. All around him there were whispered inquiries, and a couple of boys actually tugged at his arm in their eagerness to learn what Mr. Wheelock had done. But Louis coolly shrugged them off. He opened his grammar book and quickly became immersed in its pages.

He had few friends at the Rice Grammar School, and since he worked long and hard at his studies now, he had little time to play with the boys his own age in Wakefield. His only real companion was an older boy named George Tompson, who lived next door to the Lists, but as Louis progressed in school he saw George less frequently.

Each morning he arose before his grandparents were awake. In the darkness of winter he lit a little oil lamp and sleepily made his way to the washstand. Often before filling the basin he would have to crack a thin layer of ice that had formed on the water in his pitcher. It did not bother him having to wash his hands and face in freezing water. He had learned from his father to adjust to abrupt changes of temperature.

Even so, he dressed quickly to avoid a chill, jumping into clothes his grandmother had laid out the night before. Sometimes the house was still silent when he left it. His books were tied together with a leather strap and he tucked them under one arm as he made his way down the mile-long road to the lighted railroad station. Once in Boston he walked a mile to the little café where he always ate breakfast, and from there another mile to school.

This was his routine and Louis found nothing strenuous about it. He had walked long distances before in all kinds of weather, and though he had not always attended school with eagerness, he had never before had such a firm goal in mind. If he needed an education to become an architect, then an education he would have.

In June 1870 Louis completed the eighth grade and graduated with honors from the Rice Grammar School. He beamed proudly as his diploma was presented. It was the first one he had ever received, and though he would spend many more years in school, it was the only diploma he would ever earn.

III

A YEAR AT TECH

BOSTON'S LATIN SCHOOL and English High were brother schools, and they occupied neighboring buildings. Louis did not follow in his brother's footsteps when he decided to continue his schooling in the East. He attended English High, even though its academic standards were a little less lofty, for he felt it would be a waste of time for an architect to study Latin. He passed the entrance examinations with relative ease, and the school accepted him for the fall term of 1870. When he arrived, he was assigned to a drab room on the second floor presided over by a "master" named Moses Woolson.

The room was noisy on that first day. An appointed student monitor was busily calling out names of each of the forty boys in the class and directing them to desks arranged in long rows. During all the confusion and shifting about, Louis kept his eyes on the master. Mr. Woolson was a spare, weather-beaten man who might have been mistaken for a New England farmer. He had a narrow beard and unruly hair that he apparently brushed on rare occasions. His gaze was indifferent as he scanned the room, and he seemed not to care that the boys were fidgeting and joking rudely among themselves as they took their seats. The noise level in the classroom continued to rise until the monitor's high-pitched voice took on a pleading, exasperated tone. But, seated on a raised platform at the side of the room, Mr. Woolson remained placid, idly picking his right ear.

When the class was in order, the master nodded to the monitor and rose to his feet. Gradually the hubbub ended. Mr. Woolson was not tall, and he lacked the angry manner the boys had come to expect from teachers. Yet though he spoke softly, his speech was firm and conviction rang from every word. He talked for several minutes, pacing back and forth with what Louis remembered later as pantherlike movements.

"You have come here to learn," he began, "and I shall see that you do. . . . You are here under my care. *I* rule here. *I* am the master. You are wards in my charge, and I accept that charge as a sacred duty. I shall give you all that I have, and in return I expect each of you to give all that you have to me." He went on to speak of the need for discipline, for silence in the classroom, for strict attention, and he looked the boys squarely in the eye as he spoke.

"As students of mine," he said, "you will each learn to listen with your whole mind, not just part of it, and with your whole heart." He concluded by stating that he would push his students to the peak of their capabilities and even beyond. Then he gave them their first homework assignment and dismissed them for the day.

The boys were frightened as well as awed by Mr. Woolson, but Louis was overjoyed. Here indeed was a *man* — a commanding individual with an unshakable sense of purpose, a man who would lead and, by his strength and authority, be followed. Louis's regard for the master grew even greater in the days ahead. For in Moses Woolson he saw a reflection of the man he himself hoped to be — not a teacher, though he would be that too someday — but an individual supremely capable of thinking and acting for himself.

Louis was never an exceptional student in high school. But under Moses Woolson he became an alert and far more willing pupil than he might have been. He followed the master through instruction in botany, mineralogy, English literature, French, algebra and geometry. It was no longer a question of which subjects he liked or disliked. He learned from Mr. Woolson's dedicated example to apply himself to all his studies — even to those he had always slighted.

Mr. Woolson abounded in nervous energy. Despite a cool exterior, he had a high-strung nature that often got the best of him and made him lose his temper. But as his students adjusted to him, they became less intimidated by his manner and more stimulated by the stiff demands he made of them. Cowed at first into agreeing with everything he told them, the boys gradually learned to speak up. Some of them politely questioned him; others argued defiantly when he said something with which they disagreed. To their delight, Mr. Woolson enjoyed being challenged and took pleasure in fanning a mild discussion into a full-scale debate.

One day during a lesson on literature Mr. Woolson made a broad comparison between the cultures of France and England. Louis impulsively rose from his seat to ask exactly what "culture" meant.

"Culture is the genius of a people," the master declared and returned to the text of his lecture. But Louis remained standing, still puzzled.

"Sir," he persisted, "what do you mean by 'the genius of a people'?" The classroom was still. The students were apprehensive, for Mr. Woolson was often impatient when his lectures were interrupted. But at such moments when the desire to communicate was strong, a calm embraced him, and his patience knew no limit.

He looked at Louis for a moment, then stepped down from the platform, for he made a point of never talking over his students' heads. The genius of a people, he said, has nothing to do with their intelligence. It is their way of expressing those qualities of heart and mind that are part of their makeup from birth. "The culture of a people," he said, "is a reflection of their innermost selves — as individuals and as members of a race or nationality. It is the sum total of everything they are, everything they do."

Louis sat down feeling as though his mind was a cup that had been filled to overflowing. Other questions came to him, but the master's lecture took a rapid turn, and Louis was left to ponder them himself. Was there an American culture? he wondered. What had the genius of the American people produced that expressed their innermost selves? He never voiced these questions in class, but for a long time he wondered how Mr. Woolson might have answered them.

For Louis, Moses Woolson set a standard against which every future teacher would be measured. Yet he did not have a great fondness for the master, only admiration and respect. His affection was reserved for his family, and especially for his grandparents, whose farmhouse had always been more of a home to him than any place he had shared with his parents. He had come to depend on the Lists not only for food and shelter but also for understanding and encouragement. That dependence would be shaken now, for early in 1871 Grandma List became ill and was confined to her bed.

As far as Louis knew, this was her first illness, but it was not a minor one. From the depth of concern that his grandfather showed, Louis soon realized that her condition was serious. He had to accept the painful fact that she would probably not recover.

The house in Wakefield was somber and quiet, touched by gloom and a sense of foreboding. Doctors appeared frequently at the door, their faces drawn and as weary as Grandpa List's. Louis heard their whispered talk in the hallway and the soft sound of Grandma's bedroom door being opened and shut. But no one spoke to him about her, and he was not permitted to enter her room until many weeks had passed.

One day Grandpa stood by the bedroom door, his eyes glazed and red, obviously from crying. He motioned for Louis to go inside and squeezed the boy's shoulder gently as he passed. The room was bright now. The window shades had been left up for the first time since Grandma had been ill. He saw her lying rigid under the smooth bedclothes. Her face was like an ivory mask, and when he kissed her forehead the skin was cold to his lips. He turned away and quickly left the room. His grandmother was gone now, a memory to be kept alive by those who loved her.

For Grandpa List this memory became a heavy burden. "Louis," he said one day, "I must leave this house."

"Why, Grandpa?" Louis asked.

"There's too much of your grandmother here," he replied. "I can't think of staying now that she's dead."

"What will you do?" Louis wanted to know.

"Well, I've decided to sell the farm," he said. "Your Uncle Julius has asked me to come and live with him in Philadelphia."

Louis's eyes widened, and he could feel the color drain from his cheeks. Grandpa List smiled reassuringly. "No, my boy, I'm not about to abandon you. You're welcome to come with me, but your parents prefer that you stay near Boston, because you're doing so well at English High School. The Tompsons say they'd be happy to have you stay next door with them."

"Will I be able to see you . . . sometimes?" Louis asked.

"Why, of course. Why shouldn't you!" his grandfather exclaimed. "There'll be plenty of time for visits — in the summer, or when you're out of school. But right now it's best for you to be here."

In the days ahead, Louis systematically collected and packed his belongings. He was all ready to move by the time Grandpa List had sold the farmhouse and the acreage around it. He felt forlorn and empty as he said goodbye to the old man, but in a matter of days his lightheartedness returned, for life with the Tompsons proved agreeable and pleasant. Years later Louis would gratefully recall how much he owed this family. Not only did they make him feel a part of their household, but they warmly shared with him their great, consuming love of music. Through the Tompsons he came to appreciate the marvels of musical technique as well as the enchanting beauty of a musical score.

The Tompsons' son George, who had been Louis's playmate through the years, was a railway engineering student at the Massachusetts Institute of Technology. Louis rode the train to Boston with him now and then, but he generally saw less of George than he did of the elder Tompsons. It was not from George but from the young man's father that Louis learned something of the structure of musical chords, the major and the minor sounds, and the intricate variations on each. Louis always knew when Mr. Tompson was pleased with something, for the man invariably gritted his teeth. And he gritted them often, with obvious relish, while acquainting Louis with some of the great oratorio music he knew and loved. He looked forward to having Louis sit attentively beside him on the piano bench as he played and sang.

Louis's joy at hearing the oratorios was furthered by the realization that they represented yet another facet of man's vast power to create. For incredible as it seemed to him, the composers whose works filled him sometimes with joy, sometimes with sorrow, had made up their glorious music *out of their heads*. He was beginning to sense the scope of man's creative spirit.

Returning to high school in the fall of 1871, Louis was assigned to a classroom whose master — a sub-master in this case — was named Mr. Hale. He was a gentlemanly fellow, good-natured, but to Louis's eye conventional, and not nearly as stimulating as Moses Woolson. It was depressing for Louis to have advanced so far in one year — only to be allowed to drift right back. Once again school became an episode to be endured, and Louis knew he was standing still, making no progress.

He began to feel the lure of the West, as letter after letter from his brother spoke glowingly of Chicago. No more did Albert reflect on his love of the sea. Instead he wrote, "I am so happy in this place that I am thinking of going into some kind of business." When a great fire destroyed most of Chicago later that year, Louis felt an impulse to quit school and rejoin his family, but a letter from his parents assured him they were safe and all was well. Furthermore, they seemed satisfied that he remain in the East and continue his studies.

Bored and bitter by summertime, Louis wondered aloud to

George Tompson how he would be able to stand two more years of such tedium. "Why don't you try to get into Tech?" George suggested, thinking of M.I.T.'s highly respected school of architecture.

"How could I!" Louis exclaimed. "I'm not out of high school yet."

"So what," snapped George. "You don't need a diploma to go to Tech. All you have to do is pass the entrance exams, and I don't think *you* would have any trouble doing that." George was four years older than Louis and one of the few persons whose advice he trusted. So it took little persuasion for Louis to agree to submit his application, and he passed the examinations easily.

Entering Tech in the fall of 1872, he was struck by the contrast between his new surroundings and the high school he had left. There was more freedom at Tech, and the atmosphere seemed more relaxed. There were no required hours of study or class attendance. Every student was on his own — to work as hard as he wished. Of course, it was assumed that since a student was there by choice he would apply himself diligently and absorb as much as he could. Louis knew by then that he *could* work hard if properly stimulated. Since architecture was his chosen field, he thrilled to the new horizons of learning he was certain lay ahead.

Though his interest was intense, he was somewhat disadvantaged at Tech. Being barely sixteen, he was pitted against young men two and three years his senior, many of whom had already experienced a taste of college. Louis was still a round-faced adolescent, and he tried hard not to seem out of place. His only recourse was to imitate the older boys, allowing his sideburns to extend almost down to his chin, and forcing himself to swagger the way it seemed they did.

The age difference partly explains why he developed few friendships at M.I.T. Also, since he traveled back and forth from Wakefield every day, there was little time for him to indulge in a college social life. Besides, he said, he was more interested in learning architecture than in making friends.

Since 1916 M.I.T. has occupied 115 acres that stretch a full mile along the Charles River opposite Boston. But in Sullivan's day the institute was confined to a single building situated several blocks west of downtown Boston in what is called the Back Bay. This district had been nothing but mud flats and tidal marshes

The Rogers Building on Boylston Street housed M.I.T. for sixty years, until the institute moved from Boston to Cambridge.

until about 1850, when it was filled in for land use. After that the city began expanding into it rapidly.

M.I.T.'s school of architecture comprised a spacious drafting room, a library and a lecture hall. There were thirty students, all at work under the guidance of a leading Boston architect, William Ware. Once Louis had adjusted to the school, he devoted himself faithfully to his studies. He became aware that he possessed a natural talent for drawing. And he learned to comprehend and sort out the complex architectural vocabulary that would soon be his second language. But other aspects of his training were not so eagerly grasped, for day by day Louis was developing an enormous resentment of his instructors.

Professor Ware was a bland, grayish-haired man with the manner and bearing of one who had been soberly middle-aged all his life. He had an uncommonly high regard for architectural traditions, which prompted Louis to describe his teaching methods as strictly "old school." Mr. Ware's assistant was a young Frenchman named Eugène Letang, a lean and bearded fellow who spoke English precisely but lacked what Louis had come to regard as a professorial appearance. Letang had studied at the École National des Beaux Arts in Paris, a world-famous school of fine arts. Like Mr. Ware, Letang was governed by a reverence for traditions when it came to teaching architecture. But as far as Louis could tell, the only traditions that seemed to concern Letang at all were those he had been exposed to at the École des Beaux Arts. Letang considered them a kind of gospel to be followed blindly and without modification.

Because of these two men, the school maintained a purely classical point of view. Louis found this disturbing, for it suggested that architecture was simply a rehashing of old ideas. He wondered why, for example, architects should continue to imitate Gothic structures built in Europe in the Middle Ages — or attempt to reproduce the vast columned temples that had ennobled architecture in ancient Greece. Times had changed, certainly, and so had man's building needs.

That magnificent Greek temple called the Parthenon had been built in the fifth century B.C. with the only tools in existence. Standing now in ruins on a hilltop in Athens, it symbolized a Greek concept of structure that no longer necessarily applied. To Louis the Parthenon was not a building but a monument, a fragmented reminder of a culture that had risen to incomparable heights and died. Was architecture also dead? he wondered. Why did architectural forms and standards have to be modeled after those of the past? Why should a modern architect have to draw entirely from antiquity to design structures meant to respond to the needs of the present?

Dozens of such questions spun in Louis's brain as he sat day after day, listening to the flat droning voice of Professor Ware. But he remained silent; he doubted that Professor Ware was far-seeing enough to understand his queries. The man seemed boxed in by years of narrow thinking. And unlike Moses Woolson, who had been a superior teacher in every way, William Ware had no interest in how his students reacted to him. Worse, he was unconcerned by their obvious lack of concentration. He never looked at them directly as he lectured, for if he had he surely would have noticed that many of them were involved in a continuous and lively exchange of spitballs.

Louis did not engage in classroom high jinks, but his thoughts often strayed, and his gaze shifted to the windows and to what lay beyond. Invariably his vision focused on the massive stone tower of the Brattle Square Church, which was then being built. The architect, an American named Henry Hobson Richardson, had been a student at Harvard when Louis was born. From Harvard he had gone on to study at the École des Beaux Arts. But in contrast to men like Eugène Letang, Richardson seemed to have returned from Paris with a less formalized view of architecture.

What attracted Louis to the Brattle Square Church and to the other buildings Richardson later designed for Boston was his *new* use of traditional forms. Richardson was not an imitator of styles but a modifier. While in Europe he had developed an affin-

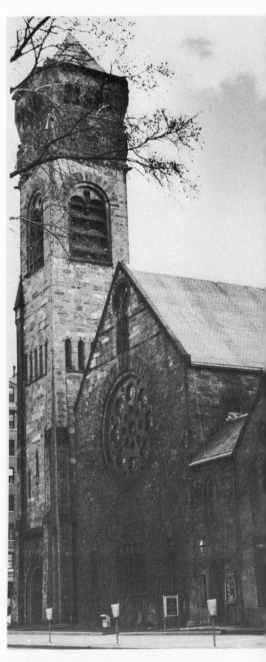

The Brattle Square Church, now the
First Baptist Church (above), was the
most impressive early work of Henry
Hobson Richardson (left). It was also
his first distinctly Romanesque design.
Even before the church was finished,
its tower, adorned with sculptured an-
gels, had become a Boston landmark.

ity for an architectural style that evolved during the Middle Ages and contained elements of ancient Roman architecture. Called Romanesque, this style was marked by rounded arches, rough stone surfaces and simple, sculpted ornamental trim. Richardson's buildings were made up of traditional Romanesque elements that he had refined and adapted to suit his own ends.

Louis grew to respect Richardson not only for his splendid buildings but also because, though influenced by a specific style, his architecture was his own. Richardson's designs had obviously come from his head, not from the handbook of architectural elements that Louis was being taught to use. Richardson's refusal to subscribe to current architectural conventions heightened Louis's own discontent. He thought to himself that Richardson, of anyone, was closest to creating a recognizably original style of architecture in America — one that might have owed its origins to other times and other cultures, yet honestly reflected the genius of the American people.

But there was little time for Louis to indulge in theorizing; the demands of the architectural school were constant. He was kept busy working on projects supervised by the careful eye of Mr. Letang and criticized in scholarly fashion by Professor Ware. However, his dissatisfaction with the instruction at Tech became greater and greater. He complained bitterly to George Tompson, whom he happened to meet on the train going home to Wakefield. "If I were in Paris, I'd be getting the original," he insisted, "not a watered-down imitation."

"Don't be too sure," George cautioned him. "How do you know Letang isn't giving you the best of what's being taught abroad?"

"Maybe he is," Louis conceded, "but the Beaux Arts is a bigger school with many more teachers. There *has* to be more to architecture than what Letang lets us do, or what Professor Ware says in lectures. After all, look at Richardson!"

George looked sharply at Louis for a moment. "Do you really want to be an architect?" he asked. "Are you sure it's the right field for you?"

"Certainly," was the reply.

"Then you'll probably have to go to Paris," said George. "Will your family provide the money?"

"Some of it, I guess," said Louis. "The rest I'll have to earn myself."

"Why don't you get a job with an architect? You know, even if you do nothing but sweep floors —"

"I'd *never* do that!" Louis interjected.

"But even if you had to," George persisted, "you'd have a better idea of what it's like to be an architect. Who knows? Maybe you'll change your mind after all."

"I'll go to work," said Louis thoughtfully, "but I won't change my mind." At the end of the school year, he left Tech, determined that he would eventually get to Paris, that he would first find a job with a reputable architect and that he would never, as long as he lived, sweep floors.

IV

TO THE WEST

IT SEEMS like yesterday when my grandson was a little boy. Now here he is, almost a man, standing at my door." Grandpa List chuckled in mock disbelief as he helped carry Louis's bags into the comfortable house he shared with his son Julius in West Philadelphia. "Will you go to school here? Your letter didn't say."

"No, Grandpa, I'm going to get a job. I think I can learn more about being an architect by working for one."

"But your education!" Grandpa List exclaimed. "You didn't finish high school, and now you've quit college after only a year."

"Someday I'll go to Paris and study there," said Louis. "But I'll have to have money. If I can work awhile and live with you and Uncle Julius, maybe I can save a little of what I need."

"Of course you're welcome to stay here," Grandpa List assured him, "but I don't know anything about the architects in Philadelphia."

"I do," said Louis. "I've heard about a man named Frank Furness."

"Is he a good architect?" Grandpa asked.

"I don't know yet," said Louis, smiling, "but it won't take long to find out."

Once settled in the house with his grandfather, Louis made his first survey of Philadelphia, a city as rich in history as Boston but more than two times as large. Louis studied the downtown section on foot, street by street, examining the buildings he passed and the details of their architecture. Little of what he saw of recent vintage impressed him very much, but one residence, still unfinished, caught his eye. Its design was fresh and distinctive, unlike the buildings that surrounded it. And most important of all from Louis's standpoint, it had a warm, inviting quality. Stopping a workman, he learned that the firm of Furness & Hewitt had designed the building.

"Would that be Frank Furness?" he inquired. The man nodded. That was all Louis needed to know. The next morning, dressed in his Sunday best, he presented himself in the Furness & Hewitt offices on the top floor of a new four-story building not far from Independence Hall. He said he had come to see Mr. Furness. An assistant asked the nature of his business, and Louis boldly stated, "It's personal." The assistant turned and gestured for Louis to follow.

Inside the private office of the firm's senior partner, Louis felt a pang of stage fright. The man behind the huge oak desk wore a menacing expression that was accentuated by his crinkly red beard, and he swore violently when he saw that his visitor was so young. "Well, what do *you* want?" he finally demanded.

Louis stifled his fear and looked coolly at the older man. "I've come to join your firm, Mr. Furness," he announced. "I've seen some of your work. I know you're a good architect."

"And how do you come to judge *my* work?" Furness inquired. "What kind of experience do *you* have, young man?"

"Well," Louis began slowly, "I've just spent a year at Boston Tech, and —"

"At Tech!" the architect cried, and then he exploded, railing against college professors and audacious young men who thought they knew everything just because they'd been to school. "You're a fool!" he bellowed, finally. Then he scowled like a bulldog. "Worse than that," he continued, "you're an idiot — to have wasted your time in such a place, letting a lot of babbling professors fill your head with rot and nonsense!"

"But I've quit school," Louis reminded him. "I want to work now. I know that's the only way I'll ever learn anything."

"Then you *don't* know anything, do you?" said Furness. By now the heat of battle had begun to affect him. He wiped his forehead with his sleeve, then removed his bright plaid jacket and flung it across a corner of the desk. "You have nothing to offer but contemptible conceit, have you?"

Louis ignored the question, if it really was a question. He agreed that he was relatively ignorant but insisted that he was bright and willing enough to learn, and that in an office run by a man so obviously gifted as Mr. Furness, he would certainly have no trouble absorbing a great deal.

Furness took a sharp breath, as though to shout or curse again. Then for just a moment he was silent. How rare it was that anyone had the courage to answer when he went into his rages. Yet this young man, so insistent and so self-assured, could stand up to him without betraying a jot of fear. Was it impertinence, stupidity or genius? he wondered. Furness was becoming intrigued.

"If it's an education you've come for, there should be no question of my paying you a salary. Is that correct?" he asked, leaning into his tilt-back swivel chair.

"No, not a salary," said Louis, "only an allowance. I won't work for less than ten dollars a week." After some quick calculation on a small scratch pad, Furness gave in grudgingly but without an argument. Louis sensed the trace of a smile widening behind Furness's thick beard, but there was not a glimmer of warmth in the man's eyes as he looked at Louis.

"You can start tomorrow," he announced, "but strictly on a trial basis." Louis extended his hand, but Furness pushed it aside reaching for his jacket. "If you want my opinion," he said, curling his lip, "you won't last a week."

His prediction might well have come true if Louis had not come under the gentle tutelage of Hewitt's younger brother John, who was the drafting room foreman. A husky, soft-spoken man, John sensed in Louis the ability to become a fine draftsman. With John's patient guidance the boy learned quickly to retrace a complex set of plans, and to do it neatly and accurately. Word of his aptitude must have reached Frank Furness, for the senior partner stopped by Louis's drafting table at the end of his first week. With customary brusqueness Furness declared, "You may stay on another week." A week later, his manner subdued, he told the boy, "You may stay as long as you wish."

Louis had proved himself, just as he was sure he would. But instead of settling down now to a quiet routine, he began working all the harder. Paris was still his objective but he wanted to learn as much as he could before he went there. And he knew that in Frank Furness he had the best possible teacher. He delighted at the speed with which Furness could produce a handsome free-hand drawing, and he was always astonished to see that the man could continue swearing and drawing at the very same time.

Most of all, Louis admired Furness's integrity, the fact that he insisted on originality from those who worked for him. In this respect he differed from his partner, George Hewitt, a tense un-smiling fellow who seldom spoke and seemed about as colorless as his pale complexion. Hewitt was a clean draftsman, but to Louis's critical eye the buildings he designed were dull, composed of hardly more than borrowed themes. Louis could never understand why Furness tolerated Hewitt; he was convinced that while Furness, like Richardson, made up buildings out of his head, Hewitt simply made them up out of books.

Louis could easily ignore the unfriendly Hewitt, for it was Furness's work that he respected. And it was this cantankerous man who put into words a principle that Louis himself had embraced — without really knowing it — when he first became interested in architecture. Furness declared that a building should *proclaim its use*, rather than disguise it. For example, a modern bank should not look like an ancient Roman temple, and a rich man's house should not resemble a medieval French castle. The idea seemed utterly logical to Louis.

His eagerness to learn was not only expressed through hard work at the drafting table; he also spent several hours in the public library each night and sat up beside his bed until very late,

Though Frank Furness was not a major architect, the exuberance and individuality of his style won Louis Sullivan's admiration. The Provident Life and Trust Company Bank of 1879 (left) and Guarantee Trust and Safe Deposit Company of 1875 (below) were two of Furness's most distinguished buildings. By 1960, both banks had been torn down.

reading everything he could find about architecture. He finally moved out of his Uncle Julius's house and took a rented room in downtown Philadelphia. Now he would be nearer the office and would have to spend less time traveling each day.

Summertime in Philadelphia was hot and uncomfortable, but the only outdoor recreation Louis found time for was an occasional Sunday walk in Fairmount Park. Its rolling, wooded landscape reminded him of the wilderness he had played in and loved as a child in Wakefield. He visited his grandfather now and then, but most of his free time was spent with books or at his drafting table in the office.

One steamy September day Louis became conscious of a strange murmur rising from the street below Furness & Hewitt. The sound was barely audible at first through the normal din of Philadelphia traffic. But it began to swell until within minutes it became a roar. Soon the entire staff joined Louis at the windows, peering down anxiously at the scene below.

The sidewalks were jammed with frantic men, some of them shouting wildly, and in no time the crowd poured over the sidewalks and milled about in a thickening mass in the street. The crowd seemed biggest outside the banking house of Jay Cooke & Company. As Louis and other junior architects cupped their ears to the noise and craned their necks, they saw that the doors of Jay Cooke & Company were shut and its shades were pulled down. Anguished cries of protest issued from the men trying to force their way into the bank, but even if they had been successful, there was nothing left by then. Jay Cooke, it seemed, had failed.

In the days that followed, panic replaced logic in financial circles. That a respected and presumably sound banking house like Cooke could founder sent streams of frightened account-holders to their banks to remove life savings. In those days, before the protective Federal Reserve System existed, no bank could survive such a run on its resources.

What caused Cooke to fail? Too many wildcat speculators —

gamblers in railroad construction and other new enterprises —
were losing money and withdrawing or borrowing funds to pay
back debts. Finally in 1873 a financial picture that had grown
increasingly shaky since the Civil War was suddenly shattered.
The panic spread to major cities across the nation and a depression followed. Many of the country's leading financiers found
themselves penniless overnight as bank after bank collapsed from
depleted funds. Men became more guarded with their money, and
banks that had survived the panic became more and more reluctant either to lend cash or to extend credit.

For a while there was plenty of work for the Furness & Hewitt
staff, but the hum of activity dimmed as the weeks passed and
few new jobs came in. Louis finally left the company in November, for by then there was practically nothing for him to do. He
was the firm's youngest member and its most recent addition. It
seemed logical and fair that he be the first to go, and he left with
few regrets. He had learned much in the months he had worked
there and would always feel grateful to Frank Furness for having
hired him. But an incident involving George Hewitt, which took
place a few weeks before his departure, had convinced him even
then that he would have to terminate his stay.

Louis kept a habitually vigilant eye on every design that was
produced in the office, eager to analyze at his leisure anything he
considered notable or unique. He dared not take any drawings
home at night, so he returned to the office to study them after
dining in a downtown café. One night while he was tracing the
intricate ornamentation on drawings of a Masonic temple that
Hewitt had designed, the architect himself burst in unexpectedly.
He had been on his way home from the theater, and seeing the
flicker of lamps in his office, had come up to see who was there.

Though startled by the visit, Louis matter-of-factly explained
what he was doing, but the explanation seemed small comfort to
Hewitt. "Those drawings are the property of this office," he said
crisply. "You should have asked permission before you came here

after hours — and certainly before you even thought of touching the drawings. I myself do not enjoy having my work *copied*." Then he left, banging the door behind him.

To Louis the idea of copying anything Hewitt had designed was unthinkable. Why would anyone copy something that was itself just a copy? He had only wanted to study the patterns of Mr. Hewitt's design at home, and compare them with others he had seen in books. He said nothing, however, shouldering the reprimand without an excuse or apology. But in the weeks that followed, as the effects of the panic of 1873 became pronounced, the tension between Louis and Mr. Hewitt was more and more apparent.

Frank Furness was still the only architect in Philadelphia whose work appealed to Louis. So once he had left Furness & Hewitt, he had no choice but to leave Philadelphia, too. At that point there was only one place he wanted to go and that was Chicago. His brother's enthusiastic description of life there, of the promise and opportunity that lay around every street corner, made the city irresistible. He packed his few possessions, left his rented room and said goodbye once more to Grandpa List. On the train ride west Louis proved as avid a sightseer as he had been as a child on his first long trip. He reached Chicago the day before Thanksgiving.

Andrienne Sullivan was happier than she had been in years on that Thanksgiving Day in 1873, for by a stroke of good fortune both her sons were in her home again. Patrick Sullivan, on the other hand, chose to conceal whatever joy he felt. He was more eager to boast of his success in the great midwestern city — and eager to assure his younger son that despite the panic, the people of Chicago still wanted to learn the latest dances. Business, he declared, had never been better.

Although pleased to hear that his father was doing well, Louis was more impressed by how grown-up his brother seemed. At nineteen Albert was something of a giant: tall and strapping. He worked in the machine shops of the Illinois Central Railroad, where Louis had no doubt he too was doing very well. Railroading had suddenly found its way into Albert's blood, just as Chicago had gradually crept under his skin.

Louis found the city to be just what Albert had described. Though it had been shaken by the panic and was still scarred by the fire, its vitality seemed unimpaired. Louis covered the city on foot, the way he had explored Boston and Philadelphia. He was surprised at the progress that had been made since the fire. But much remained to be done. And much of what had been done was not done well. This was apparent in the streets themselves, many of which had been relaid too quickly over mushy, muddy surfaces that oozed through cracks in the hardened pavement.

Very few of the hastily-built structures in the city were particularly good. There had not been time, at first, to consider producing distinguished architecture. But one new building stood out from the rest. It was the Portland Block, and from the looks of it Louis concluded that the man who designed it had been both skillful and conscientious.

The Portland Block was a four-story building made of brick and sandstone. Its architect was William Le Baron Jenney, whom people called Major Jenney, for he had fought as an officer in the Civil War and marched through Georgia with General Sherman. Louis called on Jenney and found him to be a jovial man, with hanging jowls and billowing girth that attested to his love of food in plentiful quantities. He looked at Louis through large eyes that seemed about to pop, but his look was kindly and not indifferent. Unlike Frank Furness, he was flattered that Louis had singled him out among Chicago architects and impressed that Louis had spent a year at Boston Tech. It took little persuasion for him to agree that Louis should become a member of his firm.

Major Jenney was an engineer at heart. He had sound and sometimes ingenious ideas about structure, and he appreciated fine draftsmanship. But the creative energy Louis had esteemed

Before 1871 most buildings in Chicago were made of wood.

Even major streets had structures as flimsy as stage sets.

The fire that began October 8, 1871, destroyed 17,500 buildings and made 100,000 Chicagoans homeless. Here, the burned city smolders beyond the charred ruins of the Rush Street Bridge.

in the Portland Block had come from others in the office — notably the foreman, John Edelmann, who oversaw the work of the design staff and was a competent designer himself.

Louis took an immediate liking to Edelmann. He was a rangy, muscular man with a thick, shaggy beard that gave him a perpetually disheveled look. In intellectual matters, though, he was orderly and precise. He had a wide range of interests and obviously knew a great deal. He also spoke a great deal. In fact, it seemed to Louis that he almost never stopped talking.

In John Edelmann, who was twenty-four, only seven years his senior, Louis saw a man who was his equal — in the depth and intensity of his thinking, in the degree to which he applied himself to his work, and certainly, too, in his brashness. So John talked and Louis listened, and through this bond they became inseparable friends.

John had theories on every subject that came to mind, all of which fascinated Louis. But what Louis found most penetrating, because it stirred his own youthful impulse to theorize, was John's insistence that the design of a building should not conceal its purpose. Whether it was a house, a barn or a factory, he said, a building should look like what it was. Its function should not be suppressed. He also declared that the inside and outside of a building should be in harmony. If these two elements did not complement each other, a building's design was dishonest.

In addition to exchanging thoughts on architecture, Louis and John attended concerts together, and often went to a gym. John was not particularly athletic, but he believed that a man should try to remain fit. In this respect he was like Patrick Sullivan, and Louis responded with some enthusiasm. He joined Lotus Place, the rowing and running club John belonged to, which was about fifteen miles south of Chicago on the Calumet River. Its members came there on weekends and participated in a variety of athletic events. Louis eventually persuaded his brother to become a member, and the three young men engaged in lively competition through the spring of 1874.

Louis may have regretted urging his more athletic brother to join Lotus Place, for Albert consistently won every event he entered, whether it was lifting weights or running the 110-yard dash. But it gave Louis satisfaction to note that John, despite his size and muscle development, always trailed the field. In truth, John could not stop talking long enough to concentrate on sport or exercise.

Louis's life in Chicago was rich and full. It pleased him to be back with his family and to have made such a stalwart and stimulating friend as John Edelmann. But he did not forget why he had quit school and gone to work, and he was still determined to attend the École des Beaux Arts in Paris. Little more than six months after coming west, he decided he had fulfilled his purpose in working for an architect. He had had enough practice for a while; it was theory he needed now.

He had saved a little money and his father agreed to supply additional funds to cover his basic needs and tuition. Now there was nothing to hold him back. After resigning graciously from Major Jenney's staff, receiving John Edelmann's cheering Godspeed and embracing each member of his family, he took a train to New York City. There on July 10, 1874, he boarded the steamship *Britannic*, which was then to make its first Atlantic crossing.

There were flowers and speeches at the dock. Elegantly dressed men and women bustled about. Horns tooted, and there was much cheering and waving of hats as the great ship pulled out of her berth. Until that moment Louis had given little thought to the idea of being in Europe, or even of crossing the Atlantic. But he tingled with excitement now as the ship's horn sounded a rumbling farewell blast. He and the *Britannic* were making their maiden voyage, and the prospects for each of them seemed buoyant and bright.

V

MR. ADLER

ONCE AT SEA Louis's spirits waned, for the days passed slowly. It was a lonely voyage; he made no friends. He spent most of each day reading or staring glumly over the ship's railing. For hours on end he scanned the misty emptiness of gray skies and choppy waters in the vain hope of spotting a black strip on the horizon that indicated land lay ahead and the crossing would soon be over.

After ten days the *Britannic* reached Liverpool and Louis happily debarked. His stay in Liverpool was brief, and though he remained longer in London, he barely began to grasp the complexities of that great city before he was on his way again. He saw few London buildings whose architecture pleased him, but as he passed such places as St. Paul's Cathedral, Parliament and the spire that housed Big Ben, he experienced the unshakable illusion of having walked into history.

The disparity between old and new that made London a living city aroused his interest, but another, more striking disparity repelled him. In the seedy Haymarket district he was continually accosted by beggars — homeless, filthy wretches whose world was the sidewalk and a doorway's shelter from the rain. To Louis the grandeur of London was undeniable, but he could never quite resolve its contrasts — between the poor and the mighty, the rich and the fallen.

He pondered London on the boat ride across the Channel and on the train from Dieppe, but the city's harsh images faded with his first view of Paris. For the aura of romance that had made Paris a city of legend inevitably clouded a visitor's eye. Paris had order as well as magnificent beauty, and it had warmth as well as a richness of human experience that appealed to Louis far more than the cold breath of antiquity he had felt in London.

He found quarters in one of the rooming houses that were popular with student artists. It was a narrow grayish-yellow structure whose sagging windows were set off rather handsomely by decorative, balconylike iron railings. His room on the top floor, reached by climbing six flights of stairs, was dark and sparsely furnished. It seemed even tinier than its actual small size because the outside wall followed the steep slope of the roof. There was only one window to let in light and air, but leaning through it Louis could see some of the architectural glory that drew artists to Paris from all over the world: Notre Dame Cathedral, the Louvre Museum and Luxembourg Palace.

Louis's Paris home was on the Left Bank, the students' section. This was often called the Latin Quarter because young people studying at colleges here were thoroughly instructed in Latin. However, it was not Latin but French that concerned Louis on reaching Paris. He had studied French in high school and had done fairly well, so he was distressed by how little of the language he remembered. As he walked about the city he made a point of following close behind Parisians engaged in conversation. His ear gradually became attuned to the distinct Parisian dialect, but the swift flow of words usually defeated him. He understood only a tenth of what he overheard, and that, he knew, was not enough.

He received an even ruder shock when he visited the American Legation. There he learned that the entrance examinations for the École des Beaux Arts were only six weeks off. These tests, to be given in French, would encompass a great variety of subjects — notably mathematics and history, in which he was weakest. His schooling had been patchy at best, but he was told that few foreigners, no matter how well educated, were able to pass the tests without lengthy preparation. When Henry Hobson Richardson, whose buildings Louis admired, had first tried to enter the school in the fall of 1859, he had failed all but two subjects, and had been required to take the tests again a year later before he was accepted.

Louis made up his mind that he would pass these tests the first time, no matter how much work was required. Hadn't Moses Woolson schooled him in the virtues of self-discipline? Hadn't he come all the way from Chicago just to attend the Beaux Arts? He would study eighteen hours a day if necessary, but he would *not* fail the tests.

Before leaving the Legation he was given a list of textbooks to buy and the name of the best mathematics teacher in Paris, a certain Monsieur Clopet. With the help of a street map he found his way at once to the teacher's studio. M. Clopet, a dark man who spoke only French, agreed to help and advised Louis to return the next day to join a group of other young men who were receiving instruction. As Louis prepared to leave, M. Clopet pointed to the books he carried and asked, "What are these?"

"Books I was told I would need," Louis said. M. Clopet took one of them, a book on descriptive geometry, leafed through it quickly, frowned and returned it to Louis with a disdainful look. He spoke slowly, for he was aware that Louis had difficulty understanding him.

"I suggest you drop this in the wastebasket," he said. "You will have no use for it here. *I* am the one who decides what books my students need, and *I* would never recommend a book like this." Louis felt certain that if M. Clopet were truly as firm and decisive as he seemed, the two of them would get along splendidly.

His anticipation was great when he returned to the studio at the time M. Clopet's class was to meet. The class had about twenty students, but Louis was the only American. In the weeks that followed, M. Clopet prodded them all equally to greater and greater industry. "You must work," he told them repeatedly. "That is what you are here for."

Louis was working harder than any of the others, for at the

same time he was industriously studying math he was also reading history and improving his French. Soon after meeting M.
Clopet he had hired a language tutor. He assured the bewildered
Frenchman that he knew his verbs and had a fair vocabulary,
but what he wanted was to learn to speak with the flair and
fluency of the man in the street. He yearned to talk and be talked
to, hour after hour, until the sound of the French language became completely clear to him and the smooth, slurred flow of
words was natural to his speech and ear.

The tutor was frightened off almost at once by Louis's demands. A second teacher was similarly scared away, but the third
one turned out to be ideal. The man was untiring and unafraid, a
witty fellow who enjoyed talking as much as Louis's friend John
Edelmann did. Like John, this tutor could take an incident, build
on it, layer it with historical anecdote, and hold Louis so en-
thralled that before long he found he could understand every
word. Louis had no religious background to speak of, but at his
tutor's suggestion he willingly attended Sunday services at the
Church of St. Roch just to listen to the sermon of a priest whose
precision, clarity and beauty of speech were considered exem-
plary.

As the days passed and his work load expanded, Louis could
feel his confidence rising. He was particularly pleased with his
progress in math, giving credit for his improvement solely to his
teacher, who achieved remarkable results without seeming to follow a specific method. There was no textbook, only M. Clopet
himself, talking, lecturing and demonstrating. Louis had previously considered mathematics abstract, detached from reality,
but to the persuasive M. Clopet, math was completely down to
earth — a simple and logical extension of man's ability to reason
for himself.

Louis enjoyed the sessions with M. Clopet and the long talks he
began having with his classmates. They were a friendly group,
but they had regarded him warily at first because of the way he
dressed. He had appeared in class wearing a flannel suit, white

canvas shoes and a white cap. In Chicago at the time this would have been considered model attire for any young man, but to class-conscious Parisians it was strictly a workingman's costume.

"You are a student now," one of the young men reminded him. "Soon you'll go to the Beaux Arts. You will have to wear the proper clothing."

When he was able, Louis did acquire the "proper clothing," which consisted of a morning coat, dark trousers, polished leather shoes, silk top hat, kid gloves and walking stick. And he allowed himself to grow a short beard that met and merged with the long side-whiskers he wore. Studying himself in the mirror each morning, he could not help recalling the elegantly dressed architect he had once seen on Commonwealth Avenue, and he wondered if he would ever achieve the status he was sure that man must have had.

Louis's rigorous schedule kept him from seeing much of his classmates away from M. Clopet's studio. He had little time then to sample the bohemian life for which Paris was famous — the parties, the cafés, the wine. Each night he sat alone in his rooftop retreat, a lighted candle at either end of his desk. He drank thick black coffee to stay awake and used a wet towel, which he dabbed at his face or wore like a cool turban, to keep himself refreshed.

He studied the notes he took in class; he read passages in his history texts; he practiced speaking French, conversing with himself as though his tutor were present. As the pressure of these activities increased, his brain gradually became fogged, until all the subjects he had been studying suddenly ran together in a single, undecipherable blur. It was clear that without a change of pace, he might fail the examinations out of pure exhaustion.

At the end of the third week, midway through his cram course of preparations, Louis took a three-day holiday from study. He stayed in Paris, but he slept late, enjoyed quiet, leisurely meals and visited the city's rich array of parks, museums and monuments. Thinking back, he could see how similar London was to the Boston he had once known. And now as he toured Paris he saw some of the same vitality and zest that had made him fond of Chicago. Though old, Paris appeared to possess a lighthearted spirit that kept the city ever young. Louis felt at home there, and when his holiday ended he was relaxed and rested.

A calm sustained him for the next three weeks, and he experienced no qualms or nervousness on the day that exams began. His first assignments were to complete a freehand drawing, a mechanical drawing and a simple architectural project, none of which presented too great a challenge. His only anxious moments were those he spent anticipating the second phase of testing, the oral exams. These were to be conducted in a small amphitheater and witnessed by his fellow students, all of whom were as frightened as he.

Louis's first oral exam lasted an hour, during which a stern but unassuming professor put a series of complex math problems to him as he stood waiting at the chalkboard. His anxiety decreased as his concentration heightened. He found himself thinking in mathematical terms at last, and apparently thinking clearly and well. At the close of the hour the professor took his hand and congratulated him heartily. "My boy," he said, "you have a mathematical imagination that is rare indeed."

The next obstacle, and for Louis the most worrisome one of all, was the history examination. He was comforted not at all when he learned there would be only three questions, each of a wide and sweeping nature. He had assumed there would be a great many questions, all phrased to catch him on some lapse in his knowledge of historical detail, and he had not expected that he would have to talk so much. According to examination board rules, he would have half an hour to answer each question fully. This meant he would have to talk for an hour and a half, almost without stopping. When he thought of it, he was sure he would freeze with fright and be unable to focus his thoughts. And upon entering the examination chamber, he felt a chilling sensation that his mind had become a blank.

The first question asked that he tell the history of the ancient

Hebrews, the second that he give an account of the ten emperors of Rome, the third that he discuss the life and times of Francis I, a sixteenth-century French king. Overcoming panic, Louis proceeded rapidly. His thoughts found words, and he spoke in a smooth, fluent French that flowed musically like the speech of a Parisian native-born. When the examination ended, the professor smiled, and after making Louis promise to continue studying history, declared, "I can do no less than award you the highest possible rating — and wish you a most successful future."

The ordeal was over. The weeks of work and weariness, and the sheerest test of self-discipline, had paid off. He was accepted into the École des Beaux Arts. He wrote his parents immediately to share the good news, and then plunged into the strict routine of the school he had wanted so long to enter.

To begin their training, the students of architecture were assigned to work under some of the foremost Parisian architects. Louis was sent to the studio of Emile Vaudremer, who happened to be the man under whom Eugène Letang, Professor Ware's assistant at M.I.T., had studied. M. Vaudremer's studio was a street-level workroom — drafty, poorly heated and as cluttered and dusty as a carpenter's shop. It was just big enough to accommodate the twenty students who gathered there to work on projects and hear M. Vaudremer's elaborate criticism.

M. Vaudremer was a dignified man of forty-five who encouraged his students, answered their questions patiently, but made it indisputably clear what he expected from them: absolute devotion to their work. When he was present the studio was quiet as each student applied himself fully to his tasks. But when the master left bedlam took over, and the young men began hurling insults — and anything else they could throw — back and forth. It was a studio full of talented pranksters.

At first Louis's classmates treated him like any other newcomer, making him clean the drawing boards and fetch wood for the stove. But his command of French, and his mastery of a kind of thieves' slang learned from his knowing tutor, soon raised him

in the estimation of the older students, and they accepted him as
one of them. He joined in their frivolous activities after school,
dipping generously into the night life of Paris's Left Bank. He
celebrated Thanksgiving Day by attending a masquerade ball,
dancing the can-can and staying out till after four in the morning.
Now that the greater pressures of preparing for the Beaux Arts
had ended, Paris had become a playground for him. Never in the
time he was there did the city lose one spark of its magical appeal,
but the Beaux Arts in time proved disappointing.

Early in his studies Louis realized that the school was following
a single, strict approach to architecture, treating it as a purely
problem-solving science. There was a fine sense of order to the
instruction, but that was the source of Louis's dismay. Everything
was made to fit too neatly. For every problem to be solved there
was a rule to be learned. And Louis felt that few of the problems
were at all like those an architect might actually have to face.
Science was stressed, with virtually no regard for architecture as
an art. In fact the school so pointedly denied inspiration that
Louis began to feel as though his vision were being squeezed to fit
the limits of a magnifying glass: deep, detailed and narrow.

Early in 1875, barely six months after arriving in Paris, Louis
concluded that he would soon have to leave. The Beaux Arts
simply did not offer what he was seeking; perhaps no institution
would. The school's approach was lofty, removed from life, while
to Louis architecture was as vital as a beating heart. Between
these extremes there could be no common ground.

He stayed on until spring and then made plans to return to
Chicago, happy for having been abroad but even happier to go
home. His parents were delighted to see him, of course, but his
father was particularly concerned because Louis had cut short
his training so abruptly.

"You haven't finished anything you've begun since grammar
school," Patrick Sullivan reminded him. "Perhaps if you'd listened
to me and gone into agriculture —"

"But I'm not interested in agriculture," Louis insisted.

"Well, when you start something, you've got to follow through," his father pointed out. "Look at your brother. He never stops working, or going to school either, for that matter." Indeed, Albert had been promoted to mechanical draftsman by his railroad, and wanting to rise even further, was then taking courses in night school.

Louis was unperturbed by the comparison. "School has nothing more to offer me," he said. "I know that if I ever succeed as an architect it'll be because of what I can *do*, not what I've been taught." Deep down inside, it did disturb him to recall that he had spent even less time at the Beaux Arts than Richardson had. Richardson, who was now at work on what many would call his masterpiece, Boston's Trinity Church, had run out of funds and had been forced to quit school after two years. He had remained in Paris, working for an architect for three more years, however. Though Louis's experience had not been comparable, he could content himself knowing that he was still among a small handful of Americans who had studied architecture at the Beaux Arts.

But the disappointments — and joys — of Paris faded into memory as Louis became enmeshed again in the dynamism of Chicago life. The man he was happiest to see once he was settled in his parents' home was his old friend John Edelmann. John had left Major Jenney's office while Louis was away, and had begun a partnership with an architect named William Johnston.

The firm of Johnston & Edelmann was a young, struggling organization, unable to flourish because of the panic of 1873, the effects of which were still being felt in the hard-hit building industry. It was several months before Edelmann could offer Sullivan any work, but during that period he told Louis which architects to call on to find temporary jobs that would tide him over while times were bad.

Relying on John's advice, Louis made the rounds of Chicago's architectural firms, walking many hours a day from office to office until he finally found employment. During the next few years he worked at a variety of jobs, some lasting a few weeks,

Richardson's Trinity Church appears below as it looked soon after completion in 1877. Years of accumulated grime give the facade a richer, darker texture in the modern photo above.

Side-whiskers marked Louis's emerging manhood at twenty.

some of a few months' duration. For a while he worked for Johnston & Edelmann, designing colorful *frescoes* — paintings made on wet plaster walls or ceilings — to brighten the interiors of a Chicago synagogue and a vast evangelical church called Moody's Tabernacle. But business was generally slow and commissions were few. Inevitably the partnership was dissolved. Edelmann left Chicago for more than a year, going first to Cleveland when his father died, and then to Iowa, where he tried to become a farmer. Louis was left on his own.

As he moved from firm to firm, doing journeyman work that was neither taxing nor rewarding, Louis began to shape some of the goals he would pursue as an architect. He knew he was a good draftsman; he knew he could be a tireless worker; he also knew he could not rise in his chosen field solely on the wings of ambition. He decided he would have to find an established architect worthy of his respect and then go to work in this man's firm. Eventually, he reasoned, he would become indispensable and would have to be made a partner. He had no particular architect in mind, but Edelmann, on returning to Chicago and hearing of Louis's plan, had a positive suggestion to make, a man named Dankmar Adler.

When John had first come to Chicago, prior to his association with Major Jenney, he had worked as a draftsman for the firm of Burling, Adler & Company. Now on his return he was rehired by this firm and was made its office foreman. "I want you to meet Mr. Adler," John told Louis. "You'll like him, I'm sure, and I feel certain he'll like you."

Louis nodded agreeably, but for some reason showed no inclination to pursue the suggestion. He might never have met Dankmar Adler, in fact, if Edelmann had not continually prodded him to do so. One day at Kinsley's, the lunchtime hangout of many Chicago architects, Louis decided he was tired of hearing about this man Adler. If only to silence his friend, he agreed to visit John's office that day and meet the architect.

The firm of Burling, Adler & Company occupied one large

Dankmar Adler, many years after he first met Louis Sullivan

room, bare except for an assortment of drawing tables near the windows and two plain desks in the center where the partners worked. The desks were alike, but the two men could hardly have been more different. Edward Burling, the older partner, was a middle-aged man, tall and stout. He slouched in his chair, his legs on the desk and a damp cigar jutting from between his teeth. Dankmar Adler, a man in his mid-thirties, was short, sturdily built, with a high domed forehead and massive beard. As Louis entered the office, Adler was standing near a draftsman's table.

He regarded Louis with kindly brown eyes and offered a courtly smile as introductions were made.

Adler was only twelve years older than Sullivan. Though he may have lacked some of Sullivan's exuberance, he shared the younger man's quickness of mind, ambition and drive. Their conversation was brief but lively, giving evidence that the two men had taken a liking to each other. Adler had heard a great deal about Louis and because of his high regard for Edelmann assumed that Louis Sullivan must indeed be an architect with talent and promise. Louis left the office gratified that his friend had spoken so well of him. But he did not see Adler again for many months, and after a while he actually forgot he had met the man.

John, too, seemed to have forgotten the incident, but one day early in 1879 he sent a message urging Louis to stop by for an evening chat. Louis happily obliged, for he was always receptive to the stimulating flow of talk that accompanied any time spent with John.

"Adler is leaving Burling — that's why I wanted to see you," John announced as Louis came through the door. "He's starting his own firm, and there are a number of commissions already lined up. This would be a good time for you to talk with him again."

Louis shrugged and shook his head. "Why are you so sure he would even want me?"

"More than that, I'm sure he *needs* you," John insisted. "He's a fine man. With *his* business sense and *your* imagination, you'd make a perfect team."

"And what about you?" Louis asked.

"I'm going with him, of course," said John. "I'll be his office foreman, but *you* could be his designer. He's smart enough to know he'd have to give you your head."

"Look, how do you know —?"

"Louis, I've talked with him about you. That's how I know. He's a cautious man. He's not won over easily. But we've discussed having you join the firm many times and there's no doubt in my mind that he's interested. Now, will you talk to him again?" John asked, and Louis said that he would.

John arranged a second meeting between Adler and Sullivan, and true to John's word, Adler *was* interested in Louis. The two men were cordial, somewhat reserved, but their meeting was conclusive. "How would you like to work for me?" Adler asked at last. "You would have a free hand, and if all goes well between us, *and* with the office, you should have an excellent future."

Louis glanced at John, who nodded approvingly, and then extended his hand into Adler's warm, firm grip. For Adler, certainly, as well as for Sullivan, it was a fortuitous handshake. With Sullivan as his designer, and Edelmann as foreman, managing the office, he would be free to devote more time than ever to meeting clients and to the task of bringing in new business, which was essential to the life of a growing firm. Among the new projects already commissioned were a large private residence, a theater and a six-story building called the Borden Block. There was plenty of work in Adler's office to keep Sullivan busy.

John Edelmann did not remain with the new company long. Within a year he became restless and left Chicago once more. Though neither he nor Louis knew it then, he would never work in that city again. He spent some time in Cleveland and eventually settled down near New York City. Louis wrote him often and saw him on his infrequent visits to Chicago, but John ceased being a key figure in Louis's life.

Before leaving Adler, John made certain that no new foreman was hired to replace him — and that the position was awarded to Louis. Now, as Adler's business expanded, so did the staff, and so did the scope of Louis's responsibilities, which he carried out as effectively as one who had been working in the field for many years. Adler came to rely on Louis's judgment and developed a strong liking for him. Adler had an engineer's grasp of structural techniques which Louis respected and which served to complement Louis's imaginative flights. The two men, so alike in taste but so different in temperament, worked together extremely well.

Chicago's Borden Block was among the first projects on which Sullivan assisted Adler and was also one of their first buildings to be felled by the wrecker's ball. It was razed in 1910.

One day, giving Louis a sly, mischievous look, Adler asked him, "How would you like to take me into partnership?"

Naively Louis replied, "But I work for you."

Adler chuckled, amused at how easily he had put over such an obvious joke. "Draw up a contract for five years," he directed. "The first year you'll receive a third of the profits. After that we'll split them fifty-fifty."

A partnership! That had been Louis's dream, of course, and Dankmar Adler had turned the dream into reality. Louis drew up a brief memorandum on a sheet of office stationery. Adler read it only once and signed it. He shook Louis's hand, and the partnership began. D. Adler & Company had come into existence.

Having grown considerably, because of so much new business, the firm was soon forced to find larger quarters. On May 1, 1880, D. Adler & Company moved into new offices on the top floor of the Borden Block, which had just been completed. A year later, true to the terms of the contract, the name on the door was changed to read, "Adler & Sullivan, Architects." Not yet twenty-five, Louis had attained what some would have considered the climax of a career. But for him it was only the beginning.

VI

THE GREAT AUDITORIUM

LOUIS SULLIVAN'S new prominence as an architect was as much the result of luck as of talent. It had been his good fortune to have come to the one city in America where his imagination and individualism could be thoroughly tested. Whether he realized it or not, the success enjoyed by Adler & Sullivan coincided directly with the astonishing growth of Chicago, a city that had risen phoenixlike from a depression and the ashes of a devastating fire.

Chicago's access to shipping on Lake Michigan had been a major factor, but the city's midcontinental location was also important. With railroads transporting goods and raw materials to and from the distant coasts and borders, Chicago inevitably became the nation's rail center and a hub of commerce. Lumber, coal, metals, minerals and livestock poured into the city daily from the nation's mines, mountains, rivers and plains. How dramatically Chicago changed during the peak years of the Industrial Revolution can be seen in the explosive growth of the population. Within ten years it more than doubled, rising from 500,000 in 1880 to a million in 1890, making Chicago America's second largest city.

For the architects who were still in business after the lean years of the 1870's, and for new firms like Adler & Sullivan, the boom period of the 1880's offered both an opportunity and a challenge. The demand for new construction was great, and so was the competition among architects. What evolved from this era of

The brick walls of the Monadnock Building curve inward from the base, where the structure is widest. It was described as "simple yet majestic" when it was declared a landmark.

mutual demand set a style of architectural development that would be a model of its kind for many years to come.

The most powerful impetus to construction in Chicago — or anywhere else — had been provided in 1855 when England's Sir Henry Bessemer invented a method of mass-producing steel from iron. At first confined to making the steel rails for the new railroad networks, the Bessemer process ultimately proved beneficial to the building industry as well. The ability to roll structural shapes out of iron ingots had tremendous impact on construction engineering, for steel was far stronger and more reliable than either wrought iron or cast iron.

But as late as 1880 most office buildings in Chicago were still three or four stories tall and the weight of their entire bulk was supported mainly by outside masonry walls. Because Chicago's surface earth was soft, the walls of each structure rested on a thick masonry base that lay along the entire perimeter of a building and extended several feet down into firm clay substances below the surface. This was known as a continuous foundation. At street level, where tremendous support was needed, the walls of a four-story building might be as much as three feet thick, narrowing with each higher floor as the building's weight decreased. Chicago's tallest masonry structure, the Monadnock Building, completed in 1892, is sixteen stories high. Its walls are nearly six and a half feet thick where they meet the sidewalk.

Generally building heights remained low so long as masonry continued to be the primary element of construction. One reason for this was that the cost of erecting tall buildings was considerable. Another was that the higher a masonry building rose the thicker its lower walls had to be, which meant less usable inside space on the floors nearest ground level.

A breakthrough occurred in Chicago with construction of the Home Insurance Building, designed by Sullivan's onetime employer Major Jenney. Built to ten stories in 1884 and heightened in a later addition, the Home Insurance Building was bolstered in part by an iron and steel skeleton that resembled a metal cage

The Home Insurance Building was more notable for its engineering than for its architecture. A wrought-iron skeleton supported its first six floors; steel beams bolstered the rest.

resting on a masonry base. Architects came to realize that by applying and improving this technique of skeleton construction they could erect taller and taller buildings without having to make the lower walls proportionately thicker.

Foundations were another important matter, however. A *tall* building would naturally weigh more, even with thinner walls. Because Chicago lay atop layers of swampy soil, new and sturdier foundations had to be devised to uphold the heavier structures. Adler & Sullivan's Borden Block design of 1880 had made notable progress in this direction.

The Borden Block did not have ordinary weight-bearing walls, nor was there a continuous foundation for them to rest on. The weight of the building was distributed among a series of sturdy brick columns, the *piers*. The walls between these piers were comparatively thin, because they carried only their own weight and did not contribute to the building's total support. Each pier rested on an isolated column of stone that was sunk solidly to about nine feet below ground level.

With new tools and new techniques coming into use, and a swelling backlog of projects to begin, Chicago architects could not only be assured of a livelihood but also of having untold opportunities for achieving excellence in design. But what Chicago lacked in the heady swirl of the early 1880's was a distinctive style — to apply, refine or even imitate. The savory Romanesque of Henry Hobson Richardson did not come west until 1885 when his Marshall Field Wholesale Store was begun. Until then Chicago architects — all except Sullivan — regarded him coolly.

With the Wholesale Store Richardson produced an architectural statement that the city found praiseworthy. This seven-story, block-long structure built of brownstone had surprisingly few of Richardson's earmarks. The arch theme that normally dominated a Richardson design was played down, and the facade was bare of ornament. An enthusiastic critic at the time likened the building exterior to the plain but imposing walls of a fortress built during the American Revolution. Similarly, Louis

Sullivan regarded the building as a profound expression of raw American spirit. The Wholesale Store had evolved from earlier European forms that Richardson knew, but the architect had adapted them — and blended them — to make a positive and distinctive statement of his own.

To Sullivan, moreover, the building had a personal significance. He rejoiced in Richardson's rejection of prevailing traditions that prescribed Gothic architecture for schools and churches and classical or Renaissance forms for other public buildings. And like Richardson he was convinced that the design of commercial structures should *not* be left to engineers and contractors, who had little concern for beauty.

For it was just this kind of construction — office buildings, factories, hotels, warehouses and department stores — that began to flourish during the years when electricity, the telegraph, the railroad and the rise of industrialism were having their greatest effect. And it was by designing such buildings that Louis Sullivan established his own architectural style. His approach is summed up in a phrase found later in his writings, a phrase that combines the dictates of Frank Furness and John Edelmann with thoughts that had come from his own experience: *Form follows function.*

Sullivan believed that the purpose of a building should be expressed in its architectural form, just as Furness had insisted that a building must proclaim its use and Edelmann had assailed suppressed functions in architecture. But Sullivan's theory went one step further, for he believed that the function of a building should actually determine its form. That is, if an architect sets out to design a factory, the kind of product, the size of the work force and the efficiency of output should be the architect's main considerations when deciding how the building will look. Further, he said, if the needs of a building are such that part of it must be windowless, no false windows should be cut into the facade, as was often done then to satisfy a predetermined form. Architecture, he declared, should always be truthful.

Human considerations were also linked to his theory, for to Sullivan architecture could not be considered art unless its form was satisfying. Whether a building was designed for offices or as a residence, he said, it should provide a pleasing environment for the people who use it. It should not only respond to their physical needs but should also provide spiritual and emotional comforts. To Louis Sullivan, *function* meant the whole life that went into a building.

The period from 1880 to 1886 marked Sullivan's formative years as an architect. During that time he and Adler designed nearly sixty buildings: homes, factories, theaters, railroad stations, a library, a schoolhouse, a synagogue and a clubhouse. Structural steel was not yet in widespread use, but Adler and Sullivan combined masonry with cast iron to lighten the mass of the buildings they designed. And their greatest contribution was in the design of office buildings. From their pioneer work, the form and style of tall office buildings in the 1890's ultimately took shape.

Sullivan's partnership with Adler quickened the pace of his life and removed him from many of the activities that had once held his interest. He no longer frequented Lotus Place or competed with his brother in athletics. Nor did Albert Sullivan continue making weekend sojourns to the Calumet River after 1881. The two brothers were leading separate and very busy lives. Their father could not help feeling proud of their achievements, though he never told them so. Their success exceeded anything he had ever envisoned for them — or for himself.

Patrick Sullivan celebrated his sixty-fifth birthday at Christmas time 1883, and he seemed then the strong, stern patriarch of old, unaffected by the passing years. But a few months later he was gone. He died suddenly in the little house that had served as his dancing school and as his home with Andrienne. His two sons were drawn together again, not only because of their common grief, but also because they had to look after their widowed mother. They visited her often, sharing with her the trials and triumphs of their respective careers. Within a year of Patrick's death, Albert Sullivan announced that he had become superintendent of machinery for the Illinois Central, and Louis began a project that would lead to one of his firm's most important commissions.

One winter day early in 1885, Adler and Sullivan were visited by a wealthy and influential Chicagoan, Ferdinand Peck, who had a scheme requiring the assistance of talented architects. "I want to stage a festival of opera," he told them as he removed an elegant top hat and peeled off sleek gloves. "I know of a building that would suit my purpose, but it needs a great deal of work. I've heard much about you, gentlemen, and I feel confident that *you* would remodel the place to my satisfaction."

Ferdinand Peck was a man who got what he wanted. Rarely did anyone turn down his requests — least of all a pair of architects eager to make a name for themselves in a brutally competitive profession. They told Peck they would do everything they could to please him, but privately they voiced apprehension. For the building he had selected was the huge barnlike Interstate Exposition Building in Grant Park near Lake Michigan, a site later occupied by the Art Institute of Chicago. The building had been used since 1873 for fairs and conventions, but it stood empty now. Peck was certain he could put it to good use and at the same time advance his own reputation as a man of taste and philanthropy.

Adler and Sullivan had successfully remodeled three Chicago theaters by then, so they were qualified to tackle the job. But this one, as they had suspected, was far more challenging than the others had been. The interior of the Interstate Building was simply one great open space. There was no stage platform, no stage arch, no sloping area for seating — none of the physical elements a theater required.

What the architects decided to do was erect a temporary wooden structure *inside* the existing building instead of modifying the building itself — for which there was neither time nor money. Ferdinand Peck was not interested in dipping deeply into his fortune to help the architects do their job. In fact, he was determined to spend as little as necessary in the hope that the project would come close to paying for itself.

Not only did a low budget burden the architects, but there were other economic pressures as well. The festival was scheduled to last only two weeks. In order for the theater to earn back the remodeling and production costs, it had to seat an extraordinary number of people. With this specification in mind, Sullivan designed a fan-shaped auditorium, with balconies and projecting boxes, which could accommodate 6,200 persons — all within the shell of the old, unaltered building.

Construction began in February 1885 as an army of workmen shoveled away snowbanks that had piled up around the Interstate Building, and great wagonloads of lumber were brought in. The carpenters worked rapidly under the architects' supervision, and by April 1 — an amazingly short time for such an undertaking — the new Festival Opera House was ready to open. Its stage was 80 feet deep and nearly 120 feet wide, making it one of the country's largest. As in any permanent theater, there was rigging above the stage to raise and lower scenery, and a fly loft for storing it. Dressing rooms were at either side of the stage, and a musicians' room lay beneath it. Outside the auditorium there was a grand salon where members of the audience could spend intervals between the acts eyeing each other, talking and taking refreshment.

Sullivan was responsible for the basic interior design of the opera house, but it was Adler who saw to the acoustics, the quality of the sound. The job he did was excellent, for it was said that the voices on the stage and the orchestra in the pit could be heard equally well from every seat.

Although many buildings were being wired for electricity then, Adler and Sullivan decided that an electrical system would be too costly for the Festival Opera House. Instead, Adler devised an elaborate lighting system that required 7,000 gas jets, and because the opera festival would take place in the chill early spring, he designed a steam-heating system as well. The two-week program opened on April 6, 1885, and with a total attendance of 75,000 was adjudged a great success. Its popularity suggested to Ferdinand Peck that a permanent opera house might be built and sustained profitably in Chicago.

Peck was a dreamer on a very large scale. What he envisioned now was not just a theater, for that would have been insufficient for the greater glory he hoped to receive. He wanted an auditorium building that would house within its walls a hotel and offices as well as a theater. "I want to create a cultural monument for this city," he declared expansively. And to make certain the building looked monumental, he said, it should be given an impressive tower.

Because of their work on the Festival Opera House, Adler and Sullivan were the likely architects to obtain the commission for Peck's latest dream. However, though the crusty entrepreneur had infinite confidence in the technical skills of Dankmar Adler, he had developed misgivings about the bold artistic judgment of young Louis Sullivan. Peck and his committee of fellow financiers invited Adler & Sullivan to submit proposals for the Auditorium Building, but other firms were also being considered. Committee members had grown favorable to the idea of asking Henry Hobson Richardson to submit a design, for they were impressed by the way his Marshall Field Wholesale Store was taking shape in 1885. Their disappointment was keen when the forty-seven-year-old architect became ill and died the following year, even before the Wholesale Store was finished.

Though Richardson in many ways had been a competitor, Sullivan could not help feeling a sense of loss at the passing of this architect whose work seemed to him so uniquely American — a man whose influence, more than that of any other designer, his own work reflected. But with Richardson's death Sullivan came to believe that *he* was now the foremost exponent of a native American architecture.

He took great pride in the eminence he felt, but he occupied a lonely pinnacle. At thirty he was still unmarried, and he lived by himself. His brother had been transferred recently to Cairo, Illinois, 365 miles southwest of Chicago, to be superintendent of lines for the Illinois Central. And his mother by then had gone east, where she would spend the rest of her life sharing a home with her sister in Lyons Falls, New York. Louis had moved into a house in Hyde Park, a new and highly fashionable residential district that he hoped would reflect his bountiful new status. He continued to work hard, though. Nothing satisfied him more than the profession he had chosen or the success it had brought him.

More than a dozen projects occupied Adler and Sullivan during 1886, but they kept coming back to the auditorium proposal. They were not ready to submit their drawings to Peck until the end of the year, however, and then they waited anxiously for a verdict. Initially the auditorium's exterior design called for a nine-story building with a high-pitched roof, a series of turrets and a pyramid-shaped tower that was topped by a cupola. Auditorium entrances were set off by massive arches, and the arch effect was repeated, framing each vertical row of windows.

The design may have been distinctive, but it was also ornate. Sullivan revered the simplicity of Richardson's mature work, but he insisted on encrusting his own buildings with ornament. Ferdinand Peck and the committee accepted the overall plan for the building, but preferring the simplicity they had admired in Richardson, they ordered Sullivan to strip away his fussy exterior. Normally Louis did not respond well to criticism, but in this case he had no choice but to swallow his pride, throttle his anger and return to his drawing table. His revised proposal was more contemporary in appearance and more in keeping with the rudiments of his own architectural philosophy. Gone were the cupola and the pointed roof. The tower was enlarged, and Sullivan added another floor to the main structure, bringing it up to ten stories. His revision was substantial, but still the committee was dissatisfied.

There was talk of bringing in other architects to work with Sul-

Sullivan's first Auditorium design was a grab bag of European elements at odds with his idea of pure American architecture.

The rendering for his second attempt shows a greatly simplified design concept. Still, additional revisions were needed.

livan on the final design. This would have been a humiliating slap at the young man's ego and a blow to his rising prestige. But before inviting anyone else to participate, the committee members agreed to seek advice from an expert. The man they chose was none other than William Ware, Sullivan's teacher during his year at M.I.T.

To Sullivan's delight and Adler's considerable relief, Professor Ware seemed pleased with the design they presented. He said little, merely nodding as he examined the drawings, and then he offered a scant few criticisms, one of which involved the tower. He thought it was too squat. It should be taller and more dominant, he said, and to make it more useful for office space its pyramid roof should be dispensed with. Sullivan agreed to make the changes, and Ware's report was submitted to the committee early in January 1887. The professor himself read the report aloud, after which Ferdinand Peck had some questions.

"I assume," Peck began, "that you've confined your judgment to the design at hand, merely suggesting ways to improve its details."

"That is correct," replied Professor Ware.

Peck smiled blandly. "In other words," he said, "you have made no attempt to appraise this proposal in the light of your own fine standards of design."

"I would not have presumed to make such an appraisal in this instance," said Ware.

"Quite so," said Peck, his smile fading. "Now, consider this: If *you*, instead of Mr. Adler and Mr. Sullivan, had been asked to design the building in question, would your solution to the problem have been similar to theirs? Or would you have created something quite different, something perhaps . . . *better*?"

Professor Ware thought a moment before replying. "If *I* had been engaged to design this building, I do not believe I would have had the same solution." Peck shot a triumphant glance at his colleagues. "But," Ware continued, "if I *had* arrived at something similar to what Mr. Adler and Mr. Sullivan have created, I think I would have considered it . . . the most inspired achievement of my life."

There was silence around the conference table. Peck and his partners were dumbstruck, nodding to each other in mute submission as Ware left the room. Now $1,000 richer for having performed his consultation, the professor returned to Boston, and Adler and Sullivan hugged each other for having been so splendidly vindicated. Now they could address themselves to the awesome task of carrying out their plans. At that point, Sullivan's burden was by far the greater, for the detailed execution of his design required literally hundreds of drawings. He could not do it all by himself. He had to have at least one assistant, someone who understood his approach and could produce drawings that were as precise and clean as those he did himself.

One day a slim young man, not yet twenty, with long hair and a flowing black tie, appeared at the offices of Adler & Sullivan, having heard that Sullivan needed assistance. His name was Frank Lloyd Wright. He had studied engineering at the University of Wisconsin and was now working as a draftsman for a minor Chicago architect. He was shy and unsure of himself, but the dim possibility of his being able to work in a firm as prestigious as Adler & Sullivan gave him some of the courage he lacked. Sullivan scrutinized Wright, noting how the young man's rustic upbringing was unmistakable in his manner and dress. Louis also saw in Wright something of what he himself had been when, fresh out of Tech, he had begun finding his way in the field of architecture.

When preoccupied or busy Louis tended to be aloof with subordinates and visitors alike, but on the day of Wright's first visit he was unusually abrupt. After looking at Wright's clothing and his transparently eager expression, Sullivan turned away. "I'll have to see some of your work," he said absently. "Come back Friday. Show me what you can do with ornamental details. Good day." And with that the young draftsman was brusquely dismissed.

It was then Tuesday. Wright spent the next two days and

nights filling a portfolio, making sure most of his drawings resembled Sullivan's own work very closely. Returning to the office, Wright found Sullivan at his drawing table, which he quickly shrouded with a cover-sheet as Wright approached. Without acknowledging the young man's presence, Sullivan took an armful of Wright's drawings and leafed through them. Then he turned back to his table, threw off the cover-sheet and resumed working on a lacy swirl of decoration.

Wright stood in silence a moment, not knowing whether to stay or leave. Was his work being rejected? It was impossible to tell. He made a move toward the stack of drawings Sullivan had thrust down on a shelf beside the table. Then Sullivan looked up and addressed him as abruptly as before: "You'll do, I think. You have the right touch."

Wright had earned his first glimmer of recognition. Though he went to work for twenty-five dollars a week, he advanced very quickly and was soon earning more. He grasped with ease Sullivan's graceful, elegant style. Working from Sullivan's pencil sketches, he provided nearly all the detailed drawings for the ornamentation that was applied to the Auditorium Building, inside and out. Eventually Wright became foreman of designers, supervising a staff of thirty draftsmen.

It took three full years to build the auditorium, which covered one and a half acres — an entire city block. Two hundred men and thirty teams of horses were needed to complete the project. They worked at a killing pace — and often at night, aided by electric floodlights. Construction problems at times seemed monumental, and these fell mainly to Adler, the engineering brains of the firm, whose problem-solving skills frequently approached genius.

According to the plans, the building was to have load-bearing walls made of masonry — not just the outside walls, but also those that rose between the theater, the offices, the hotel and the tower. Continuous-load wall construction called for continuous-load foundations, not isolated columns as had been used in the

Borden Block. These continuous foundations, compounded of concrete with steel and timber reinforcement, had to support more than two tons for each square foot. And the tower had to be even more firmly bolstered, for it would rise seven stories taller than the main structure and weigh an additional six or seven thousand tons.

How to support the auditorium and its tower was only one of Adler's problems. Another and far more difficult one was *settlement*. Because the ground was relatively soft and moist, Chicago building engineers usually made allowances for a slight but measurable settling or sinking of their buildings with the passing years. Adler could do nothing to prevent the Auditorium Building from settling, but he knew the main structure and the tower *had* to settle at precisely the same rate during construction.

Sullivan might have simplified the problem by separating the tower from the other units, but that would not have pleased him much. He envisioned his Auditorium Building as a fully integrated structure. Thus for the first ten stories, more than half its height, the tower was fastened to walls on three of its four sides. With these walls bonded to each other, any unequal settling would have been disastrous. Yet unequal settling seemed unavoidable.

While the tower was being built and until it reached its total height, its weight — relative to the supporting strength of its foundation — would be less than the weight pressing down on foundations lying beneath the three adjacent walls. The stress caused by this uneven downward pressure would have cracked the walls, and the building would have been structurally unsound long before it was finished.

Still, the tower had to be properly supported. What was Adler to do? After weeks of head-scratching and computation, he arrived at a possible solution: *artificial loading*. Like a fisherman using lead sinkers to weight down his line, Adler had pig iron and brick applied in bulk to each floor of the tower while the walls were going up. With this additional weight he hoped the load per

The completed Auditorium with its unornamented facade was a good example of Sullivan's originality as an architect.

square foot pressing down on the tower's foundation would equal that resting on foundations beneath the three adjacent walls. Then, as construction progressed, the artificial load was gradually reduced. By the time the tower was finished, the last of the pig iron and brick was being hauled away by workmen.

Adler's solution was undeniably primitive, but it worked! The result was as sound a piece of construction as any that had been built on Chicago's marshy soil. The Auditorium Building not only represented an engineering miracle, but as perhaps no other project it expressed the harmony in which Adler and Sullivan worked. Sullivan was the unbridled exponent of individuality in architecture, but it was Adler who made Sullivan designs work. Because

After Chicago's opera company found a new home in 1929, the Auditorium theater was seldom used. Its huge stage housed a bowling alley during World War II, and for some time afterward its hotel rooms and offices were college classrooms. Real estate men wanted to put up a new building in its place. But because it was so big and built so solidly, the demolition cost would have been enormous. So the Auditorium stood dark and neglected for many years. In 1960 a council was formed, and plans were made to restore the building. More than $2,000,000 was raised, and gradually the Auditorium's splendor began to reappear. These recent photographs show the interior of the theater: its 98-foot-wide stage (far left), its balcony and galleries (below left), its decorative ceiling arches (left). In October 1967 the Auditorium had a gala reopening (below).

of Adler's expertise and sound judgment, the several units that composed the Auditorium Building were incorporated into a massive, impressive whole — and the acoustics inside the auditorium surpassed even the superlative Festival Opera House.

In solving the engineering problems presented by Sullivan's complex design, Adler did not neglect the technical facilities required of a theater that was to be as well suited to concerts, ballets and operas as to conventions and society balls. Backstage and beneath the hardwood floor was the latest hydraulic equipment for shifting scenery and for raising and lowering various sections of the stage itself. This flexibility extended into the auditorium proper. To make it seem intimate when only a modest-size audience was anticipated, hinged ceiling panels could be lowered to cut off the top two galleries, and there were curtains to close off the rear third of the balcony. Thus, without compromising the architecture, seating capacity could be cut by nearly half — from 4,237 persons to 2,574.

The design of the auditorium interior was a triumph of Sullivan's good taste and invention. Ivory and gold were the dominant wall and ceiling colors, and the seats were upholstered in rich yellow satin. Sullivan's agile hand, and that of Wright, his assistant, could be seen throughout the house in the ornate scrollwork and the bands of lacelike stenciling. Electric lights softly illuminated the decorative patterns of Sullivan's ceiling arches — and were also recessed into the ornamentation that extended beneath the balcony and galleries and along their outer edges.

The auditorium was not completed until 1889. But enough work had been done so that, with entwined flags hiding the scaffolding and exposed rafters, it could be used for the Republican National Convention in March 1888. Benjamin Harrison and Levi P. Morton were nominated President and Vice-President there, and twenty months later, after winning the election and taking office, they were among the honored guests when the Auditorium Building was officially dedicated on December 9, 1889.

It was a gala evening. Leading opera singers performed solos, and a chorus sang a special song that Ferdinand Peck had commissioned. A thousand persons were seated in chairs on the stage, and two temporary boxes were built at the sides of the stage — one for the governor of Illinois and his party and one for the President, Vice-President and their wives.

Of all the guests, Albert Sullivan was the man with whom Louis was happiest to share the evening's joy of achievement. Back in Chicago to be his railroad's general superintendent, Albert was every bit as proud of his brother's work as Louis himself, for in many ways the Auditorium Building was unparalleled. It was ten times bigger than any project Adler & Sullivan had undertaken, and it was the largest piece of construction in Chicago at the time. In addition, it was the largest permanent indoor theater that had yet been built anywhere.

Ferdinand Peck had his cultural monument, and Chicago had a new landmark. The auditorium was also a landmark in the development of Louis Sullivan's style and the advancement of his career. Although he did not know it then, he had reached the peak of his professional life. Greater architectural achievements lay ahead, but nothing he would ever do was to bring him the kind of recognition he had earned from the auditorium.

VII

BUILDINGS THAT SOAR

LOUIS LOOKED down Michigan Avenue and squinted up at the Auditorium Building. Yes, he thought, there could be no doubt of it. The tower held its head in the air as a tower should. It was tall, majestic, as impressive in style as it was in mass. At the time of its completion the tower was Chicago's tallest structure, and it was there, to the sunlit sixteenth floor, that Adler and Sullivan moved their headquarters. Lofty as an eagle's nest, the firm's new offices gave the architects a peerless vantage point from which to view the city. All Chicago was spread out at their feet.

By now their renown had spread to other cities, for they had begun receiving commissions in various parts of the country. An opera house was under way in Pueblo, Colorado, to be wrapped in an outer layer of offices and set off by a tower. Salt Lake City wanted an office block that would be similar in style to a Chicago building Louis had designed in 1888, the Walker Warehouse. That seven-story structure, built of smooth-faced masonry, was comparatively free of decoration. Its similarity to the Marshall Field Wholesale Store expressed Richardson's influence on Sullivan as no other building could.

Louis took a trip to the West to check on the new commissions soon after his Auditorium Building had opened. He enjoyed being out of Chicago and stayed away several weeks. The Auditorium had required years of work, during which time other, similarly demanding projects had been under construction. To extend his energy through consistently long days and nights of work, Louis

The Marshall Field Wholesale Store (left) by Richardson was the forerunner of Sullivan's Walker Warehouse (above). They were similar in mass and scale as well as design, and each occupied an entire block. Commissioned in 1885, a year before Richardson's death, the Field Store advanced architecture to the threshold of the modern era. It was destroyed to make room for a garage, but the building it inspired is still standing.

had taken to drinking endless cups of coffee. Now he found it difficult getting to sleep. He was exhausted, but he could not rest. He craved a change of scene, yet he was so keyed up that it took a long time before his tension eased and he could relax.

He eventually went to California, thinking the climate and that state's fabled wonders would be beneficial. But it was January, and San Francisco was cold. San Diego, drenched by winter rains, was no better, so he headed east to see New Orleans. Louis's only memory of that colorful Old World city was of its dirtiness, but during his stay he met two Chicago acquaintances, James Charnley and his wife, who were also on vacation.

Louis was about to end his sorry wanderings and go home, but the Charnleys persuaded him to accompany them to a spot they had discovered and become devoted to: Ocean Springs, Mississippi. It was eighty miles from New Orleans on the eastern shore of Biloxi Bay. "It's such a sleepy place," Mrs. Charnley told him, "that even *you* will have trouble staying awake there."

Louis went mainly to be agreeable, but also to delay going back to work. He was not expecting miracles of Ocean Springs — which was why he was so surprised by what he found. For there, in a setting that was surely a masterpiece of nature, stood a village untouched by time. Louis's first glimpse took in the ramshackle railroad depot, a small, quaint building beside a decaying platform. From there he could see a post office, barbershop, butcher store, saloon and one-man jail — all dwarfed by gnarled live oak trees and bathed in sparkling reflections from the bay. Pigs and cows wandered through the streets as casually as the pleasant, soft-spoken villagers, and the very air had a velvet smoothness, although spiced with pine scent and the tang of a saltwater breeze.

Louis spent two weeks in this rustic idyll, luxuriating in the creaking graciousness of the town's old hotel. He accompanied the Charnleys on long walks, and together they took wagon rides into the pine and hickory forests that were choked with twisted wisteria limbs and the blooms of dogwood, azalea, magnolia and

At thirty-four, becoming famous, Louis wore a look of mature self-confidence, but there was a boyish glint in his eyes.

sloe. Eventually the three Chicagoans realized they were not alone in this wilderness. They saw a house deep in the woods, and one day they met its owner, Newcomb Clark, once a volunteer colonel in the Civil War and later speaker of the Michigan State House of Representatives. He explained that he owned a large section of the fragrant woodland that Louis and the Charnleys found so pleasing to explore.

"I'd be mighty obliged if you folks would settle hereabouts," said Colonel Clark, when he learned how much they liked the region. "I've cleared some of the land, but I need neighbors now more 'n trees. My wife gets lonely here, so far away from things."

"We'd certainly like to see the land you own," said Louis.

"It's pretty wild, now, I warn you," said Colonel Clark. "But once it's cleared of scrub pine and underbrush it'll be like living in a forest of oaks. Do you like live oak trees?"

Did he *like* them? What a question! The beauty of this woodland, beyond which glistened the bay, was incomparable. He could barely contain his eagerness to own some land, for he knew he *had* to have a house there. The Charnleys, no less ecstatic, said they too would purchase land if Louis would design their home — which he agreed to do. A deal was made, contracts were signed, and Louis quickly produced designs for two bungalows to be set three hundred feet apart on adjacent plots of land. He turned the plans over to a local builder.

Louis himself specified the amount of land to be cleared, taking pains to retain as much of the wilderness as he could so as not to despoil a setting he was convinced had been arranged by an invisible poet. He mused later that the price he and the Charnleys had paid was probably ten times what the land had cost Colonel Clark. Even so, the price could not have marred Louis's joy each time he thought of the land and contemplated a visit. Ocean Springs became his garden, his haven, his workshop, his place of inspiration and rest for the next eighteen years.

In March 1890 when he returned to Chicago, Louis found that his office had been receiving more commissions than it could readily handle. Adler, the more stolid of the partners, was cool and unruffled, taking everything in stride — the work, the pressure and the new prestige. Louis, on the other hand, did not adjust so easily, even after settling back into office routine. He worked as hard as ever, but despite Adler's calming influence he seemed to accept the prestige far better than the pressure. In June of that year he was invited to join the select Chicago Club, whose members were nominally men of means but primarily men of achievement. It was a rare honor for someone so young, and an undoubted tribute to Louis's high professional standing, but often he felt it gave him license to rage at a client's demands.

Equally successful in his own right, but far less volatile, was

Louis's cottage at Ocean Springs was surrounded by shrubbery and tall trees. It was a shingled, one-story dwelling whose steep roof was designed to deflect the sun's strongest rays.

Louis's brother. Though Albert lacked Louis's flamboyance and celebrity, his placid nature complemented Louis's temperament. Thus, despite their widely differing interests and dissimilar patterns of life, they continued to be close. They also continued to be concerned about their mother, who had recently become ill with diabetes.

Albert was anxious for Andrienne to return to Chicago, where he believed she would receive better medical attention than in a small town like Lyons Falls. Also, he felt she should be near her sons so they could keep a close watch on her. He bought a plot of

The modest residence Louis built for his mother is imposing and impressive despite its small scale. It is still standing today, but has been remodeled since this picture was taken.

land on Lake Park Avenue, not far from where he lived himself, and Louis designed a comfortable home that would provide the ideal atmosphere for her.

Because the building site was small, Louis laid out a narrow oblong that stood close to its neighbor. Extending forward from the smooth facade of the finished house was a thick ornamented cornice at the roof line and a three-paneled bay window on the second floor. The one unique element was a kind of indoor veranda on the first floor, beneath the bay window. It was a small, enclosed porch that faced the street, shielded by flowering boxed shrubs and a pair of circular columns. The veranda was such that Andrienne could sit outside when the weather was fair and still have the privacy she would have indoors — a thoughtfully conceived idea that she would have appreciated, but unfortunately never saw. Andrienne Sullivan died in May 1892, before the house was finished. Her grief-stricken sons brought her body back to Chicago for burial next to their father.

Albert had probably planned to stay in this house with his mother, but with her death he could not bring himself to live there. Not wishing to sell a home his famous brother had designed, he persuaded Louis to give up his Hyde Park residence. Reluctantly Louis brought his books, his elegant furnishings and a growing collection of bric-a-brac to the unpretentious house on Lake Park Avenue.

Although well established by now as an architect and Chicagoan of distinction, Louis Sullivan had no time for complacency. He was too busy, first of all, and second, he was working in an era of constant technological change. The 1890's were a decade that saw the end of large-scale masonry construction and the appearance of more and more tall buildings — made possible by the growing use of iron and steel, and the application of a newly developed means of fireproofing buildings by placing hollow tiles in walls and between floors. It was in this era that Adler and Sullivan embraced the new technology and brought it into its own.

As cities became crowded and more congested, the men who

commissioned buildings wanted more light and air — and, most of all, more office space. The tall office building resulted as much from economic pressure as from mechanical invention. With the rising cost of land and its decreasing availability, there was simply nowhere to go but up. What made upward expansion feasible, even before the revolution in construction methods had taken place, was the development of the passenger elevator. First used in 1857, the elevator had evolved from a clumsy, steam-powered invention by Elisha G. Otis to a less primitive hydraulic mechanism in the 1870's. Later, in 1889, Otis Brothers & Company introduced the first successful electrically operated elevator, which has been improved periodically ever since.

But what gave form and shape to the tall office building — more than the tools, technology and mechanical invention of the late nineteenth century — was the soaring imagination of Louis Sullivan. The success of the Auditorium Building, the last large masonry structure he would create, carried him into the era of structural steel and into the frontiers of modern architecture.

Sullivan's work has been classified as belonging to the "Chicago School," for Chicago was where the boldest strides in refining the new vertical system of architectural design took place. However, Sullivan's first big undertaking after the auditorium occurred not in Chicago but in St. Louis.

On visits to that city to attend professional meetings and conventions he had met Ellis Wainwright, the heir to a brewery fortune, a collector of paintings and sculpture, and an admirer of Sullivan's work. Wainwright had purchased a corner lot in downtown St. Louis, and he wanted a Sullivan-designed building on it. The knowledge, however satisfying, that Wainwright had plenty of money, superb taste and an awareness of architectural standards made it no easier for Sullivan to create a suitable — in this case, outstanding — design. He returned to Chicago and brooded while he sifted through a frustrating multitude of half-formed ideas.

Ultimately he followed the advice he often gave his staff: When a design fails to materialize, get away from the drawing board. Leave the office. Take a walk, allow your mind to roam free. Sullivan, though barely of medium height, had the long stride of a giant. His walk was almost a strut. Now as he strode importantly up Michigan Avenue a clear picture of what would become the Wainwright Building flashed into his mind. He remembered it later as having been a sudden, volcanic realization, and the image remained as he rushed back to his office to put the idea down on paper.

What Sullivan sketched in haste after this burst of inspiration was no less a revelation to the architect himself than to Frank Lloyd Wright, his foreman. Wright, whose office was adjacent to Sullivan's, would never forget the excitement he felt when Sullivan appeared in the doorway and thrust a set of rough sketches onto his desk. What Wright recalled seeing was the crude prototype of what would become the world's first skyscraper.

Not that the Wainwright Building was the first high building; far from it. In the five years since the Home Insurance Building had been finished, more than half a dozen tall structures with frames like steel cages had been erected. There was Chicago's thirteen-story Tacoma Building, for example, and the slim eleven-story Tower Building in New York. But these buildings and the handful of others put up before 1890 rose in horizontal sections like many-layered cakes — because most architects tended to play down heights. By contrast, what Sullivan created in his Wainwright Building, far from denying its height, made a point of emphasizing it.

The first two stories, finished in plain brown sandstone, provided a base for the tower that soared above it. From the third floor to the tenth or "attic" floor, the building's brick-faced piers rose without interruption like long, unbroken lines. To make this vertical statement even more pronounced, the panels that covered the horizontal steel beams between piers were recessed. Set back

The Wainwright Building, completed in 1891, began the skyscraper tradition that gave form to today's tall office buildings. Its simple design was enriched by sculptured panels of terra-cotta, and its soaring piers proclaimed its height as no other building had till then. But as time passed, the building began to look shabby. In 1966 a group of concerned St. Louis architects drew up plans to renovate the exterior and prepare the interior to accept modern heating and lighting, as well as central air conditioning.

from the piers, these ornamental panels, or *spandrels*, resembled row upon row of broken lines that complemented the clean and continuous verticals.

The Wainwright Building was never considered a departure from trend, but a fulfillment. And because the building proclaimed its height in a graceful expression of vertical unity, it set an example that was followed by architects for nearly fifty years. Adler and Sullivan followed and varied this vertical theme to great success throughout their partnership. But in their second skyscraper commission, the Schiller Building, they altered the form considerably to create a design that would fit a narrow space on a Chicago street that was already crowded with buildings.

The Schiller Building, commissioned in 1891 by the owner of a German-language newspaper, was to house a 1,286-seat theater, rooms for a large German club, an assembly hall, a restaurant and more than two hundred offices. The site acquired for this all-purpose structure lay in the middle of a block. On one side was an old five-story building; Adler & Sullivan's six-story Borden Block was on the other. Between these structures lay a strip of land that was long as well as narrow. Whatever the architects designed for the site would have to be tall in order to contain all the facilities required by the client. But to have erected a building that filled the entire site would have produced an eyesore — a building disproportionate to its neighbors and out of tune with the character of the street.

What Adler & Sullivan devised was a series of setbacks that began above the six-story level where the theater was housed. The setbacks relieved the building's mass, varied its shape and handsomely offset the great central tower that rose in a straight line from the second to the seventeenth floor. In addition to making the most attractive use of a small building site, the architects inventively provided enough open space around the building to let in the maximum amount of daylight and fresh air. Since then the architectural setback has been copied, not always with equal suc-

The Schiller Building eventually became the Garrick, and its theater a movie palace. Though the building was an architectural milestone and a Chicago landmark, it was razed in 1961.

cess, by architects in cities where building sites have become more and more cramped.

For years it has been argued which of the two partners was the more talented: the retiring, self-effacing Adler or the self-conscious, attention-demanding Sullivan. Sullivan's critics, who are many, have stressed that Adler was the genius who determined which foundations Sullivan's structures should rest on, and the acoustical wizard behind the success of the theater buildings. Furthermore, they have insisted that if Adler really *was* the one whose problem-solving ability gave birth to the setback, Sullivan actually contributed little to the partnership beyond his vivac-

ity and a fondness for ornament which not everyone would agree
was a distinguished hallmark.

There will never be a way to know for certain which partner
contributed what to the success of Adler & Sullivan buildings,
other than to assume that Adler was the engineer and Sullivan the
artist, and to distribute praise or blame accordingly. The writings
of neither man offer much of a clue. Each wrote flatteringly of the
other, for during their association a genuine bond of friendship
existed beyond their strong mutual respect.

Though only twelve years apart in age, in many ways they were
at least a generation apart in their thinking. Sullivan's outlook
was unfailingly American, and Adler remained influenced by the
restrained upbringing he had experienced in Germany, where he
lived till he was ten. Adler's father was a rabbi who had imbued
his fourteen children with "old school" standards far more traditional than Louis Sullivan ever knew. And unlike Sullivan, Adler
came to architecture purely by accident. He had an unhappy ap-
prenticeship in the mercantile business, and then because of his
freehand drawing skills he was sent to work in an architectural
firm where his interests and aptitude ultimately merged. Adler
and Sullivan were both strong-willed, and there must have been
clashes between them, but most of the time they worked in positive harmony. The proof can be seen in their achievements, as
well as in the fact that neither architect was as successful on his
own as he was in partnership with the other.

Another notable contrast between the two partners was the fact
that Sullivan was a carefree monied bachelor, while Adler was a
settled family man, father of two sons and a daughter. Not even
this difference wedged the men apart, however, for Sullivan grew
to love the Adler children and was a frequent visitor to the Adler
home, which the firm designed and had built in 1886.

Louis was a particularly welcome dinner guest on Friday, the
eve of the Jewish Sabbath. He sat, his eyes glistening, alongside
the Adler children while their mother, Dila Adler, lit the Sabbath
candles and spoke the traditional prayer. The children delighted

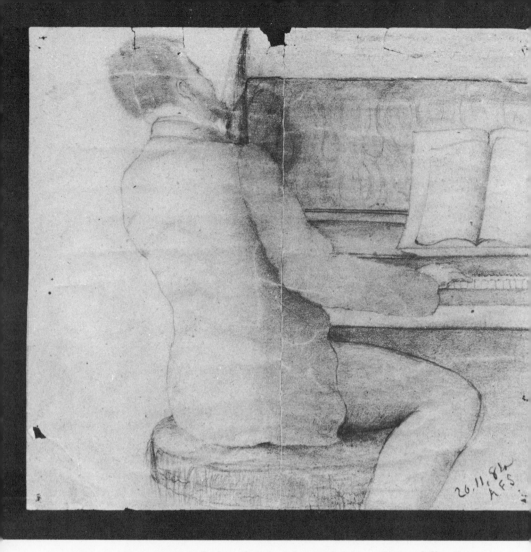

It is assumed that Louis inherited his artistic skills from his mother, whose delicate sketches he treasured. Here is a pencil drawing she made in 1884 of Louis playing the piano.

in Louis's coming, for he would entertain them with his quick freehand drawings, and then after dinner they would gather around the piano and sing, while he picked out melodies on the keyboard until it was past their bedtime. Often the children visited Louis on Sundays at his Lake Park Avenue home, eager to examine his shelves of Chinese ceramics and Indian statuettes, to tread gaily on the rare Persian rugs he had bought at auction and to admire the latest pieces of bronze and jade he had added to his collection. It was rare that they did not leave the house with a gift — something he had acquired on one of his trips to the West or the South.

As often as he could arrange it, Louis took time off to visit Ocean Springs to rest if he could, but mainly to see to the work on his shingled cottage and the care of his land. He supervised work on the Charnley house too, for it was only slightly less a responsibility to him than his own. After the cottages themselves were finished, there were stables to be built and the quarters for a domestic staff, and then Louis decided he wanted to grow roses. He read a great deal on the subject and proceeded to design an elliptical-shaped rose garden 160 feet long, with beds arranged one inside the other and separated by narrow paths. A woodland clearing would hardly seem ideal for a formal garden, but the contrast pleased Louis nearly as much as the clustered blooms.

Albert often accompanied Louis to Ocean Springs, and in 1891, through Albert's influence, the Illinois Central asked Louis to design a railroad station in New Orleans. Adler & Sullivan had plenty of work to keep a staff busy, but Louis welcomed this small commission, for it gave him an excuse to combine business and pleasure and to visit Ocean Springs more often than usual. Each time he went he worked on ways to improve the appearance of his cottage and the grounds around it, admonishing his staff to take better care of the trees and to use the lawnmowers more judiciously.

Albert enjoyed Ocean Springs almost as much as his brother did. As general superintendent of the Illinois Central, he could visit New Orleans whenever he wished. From there it was but a few hours' trip to the Sullivan cottage. Other interests brought him south fairly often, for he had become a member of the Mississippi River Levee Board, a New Orleans committee that was concerned with water and rail commerce.

Among his fellow board members was a man named Spelman, who took a liking to Albert. They talked long and earnestly about

Albert Sullivan strongly resembled his younger brother; however, their lives each took a different course.

the economic pros and cons of transporting goods by rail or river, and now and then Albert was invited to spend an evening at the Spelman home. As time passed, the conversations between the two men shifted to other more personal matters, for Albert took a liking to one of the Spelman daughters, Mary, and she quite obviously fancied him.

Mary was fair and only as plump as it was proper to be in 1892. She spoke well for her twenty-three years and seemed very much at ease having a guest in her home. The fact that she was fifteen years younger than he did not dampen Albert's interest in her. Hadn't his own parents been seventeen years apart in age? And besides, Mary was unconcerned by the age difference. She married Albert in February 1893 and moved to Chicago, settling down with Albert in a house on Kimbark Avenue.

Louis's reaction to his brother's marriage was a mixture of joy and sadness. He was glad that Albert had found a lifelong partner, but he was fearful that he and his brother might no longer remain close. The fact that from the start Mary seemed cool to her brother-in-law was natural enough, because any woman with

The charm dispensed by Mary Spelman to win Albert Sullivan as her husband was wholly lost on Louis.

her genteel Southern upbringing would have found Louis's brashness hard to bear. And, having been sheltered, she might have been expected to cast disapproving eyes on Louis's spendthrift attitude and roving bachelor ways.

But as the first months of marriage passed, Mary Sullivan's coolness toward Louis hardened into cold reserve — and then resentment. She was disturbed and annoyed by Albert's affection for Louis. She wanted her husband to herself, without having to share him with a seemingly callous brother-in-law. Albert, finding himself the unlikely object of a family tug-of-war, was powerless to bring the two opposites together, for neither side would yield to the other. Louis knew why he was no longer so welcome in his brother's house, but he was a proud man, proud of himself and his success. He did little to try to win over his sister-in-law. Not long after Mary gave birth to a daughter, the distance between the two brothers — once no greater than a handshake — widened into an unbridgeable gulf.

One Sunday afternoon Albert called on his brother unannounced, a firm, tight-jawed expression flashing a warning to

Louis that he should not expect a brotherly social visit. Louis poured glasses of sherry, which Albert refused, and then pondered as Albert sat stiffly looking around the cluttered, lived-in parlor with uninquiring eyes.

"You're happy here, I know that," Albert began abruptly. "But there are other matters to consider now." He shot a look at Louis, whose face, for the moment, remained impassive. "My daughter — she needs the best I can give her. And my wife . . ." His voice trailed off. Louis gulped his glass of wine.

"The problem is," Albert continued, "that the heating in our house is inadequate. Mary is worried about our daughter. An infant needs the best, you know, and *this* house would serve our needs completely. You understand, of course. It's for the child. . . ."

"I understand that this is your house," said Louis gently. "You own it, so of course you should live in it."

"Ah then, so it's settled," said Albert, rising.

"Yes, it's settled — permanently," said Louis. He set down his glass, turned and left the room. Despite his calm resignation to abandoning a home he had come to love, he remained shocked and deeply hurt. Obviously Mary had been behind the scheme, but why should Albert have consented to it? Why would Albert have agreed to sever the last thread of a bond that had existed for nearly four decades? The question haunted him, but he would never know the answer, for the brothers rarely saw each other after that.

VIII

THE GOLDEN DOORWAY

THE 1890's were a turbulent and disillusioning time in the life of Louis Sullivan. Not that his eminence was being eclipsed by other better architects, but his fundamental idea of a purely American style, a new architecture free from the clumsy transplanting of old ideas, would soon come to be ignored.

What engaged his energy and aroused his concern during the early years of this critical decade was the World's Columbian Exposition, a great fair to commemorate the 400th anniversary of Columbus's discovery of America. Authorized by an 1890 act of Congress, the fair was to be a showcase for cultural and industrial achievements, not only of the United States but of other nations as well. New York, St. Louis and Washington, D.C., had vied for the chance to host the fair, but intensive lobbying by Chicago's business, political and social leaders had finally won out. The actual site of the fair was Jackson Park on the south shore of Lake Michigan. There, like a pumpkin transformed magically into a glittering coach, a magnificent city was to rise from the marshes and windswept ridges of sand.

A Committee on Grounds and Buildings sought advice on planning the fair from the architects Burnham & Root. This respected partnership, which began in 1873, had contributed more noteworthy buildings to Chicago's architectural scene than any other firm — more, even, than Adler & Sullivan. And the sixteen-story Monadnock Building by Burnham & Root, then under construction, was destined to become a landmark and the last great ma-

Daniel Burnham had tried mining, then selling plate glass, before deciding to become an architect.

sonry structure in Chicago. Daniel Burnham, the firm's senior partner, was named chief of construction for the fair, and Root the consulting architect.

Like Louis Sullivan, John Root was the artistic genius of his firm, and Louis admired him greatly. In fact, Louis thought the fair would benefit by having Burnham & Root design *all* of the buildings. But that was impossible, for such an undertaking would have involved a single firm for at least ten years, and Congress had stipulated that the fair be held before the end of 1893 or not at all.

With a task so formidable and no time to spare, it was obvious that a whole group of architects would have to be employed. Burnham favored calling on the most prestigious — and, by nature, conservative — architects from the East Coast, but the Committee on Grounds and Buildings was insistent that Chicago architects be used. A compromise was finally reached and a board of architects agreed on. Its members represented five outstanding eastern firms and five from Chicago. Among the latter was Adler & Sullivan.

Collectively the committee was to plan the physical layout of

John Root, four years younger than his partner, was less ambitious but a much more experienced architect.

the fair, and each member firm would design one of the buildings. Sullivan, who would be assigned the Transportation Building, was aware that the eastern architects tended to regard the work of the Chicago School with raised eyebrows. But he had few qualms about the presence of five easterners on the board, for there would also be five Chicagoans, as well as Burnham and Root — and Root was his friend and ally. Louis knew that Root pretty much shared his views on design, and since the firm of Burnham & Root also planned to contribute a building to the fair, the balance of architectural styles could be expected to favor Chicago.

At first the easterners were reluctant to be involved in the project, fearful that a fair in Chicago would be little more than a cattle show. So, early in December 1890, the portly, persuasive John Root went east to outline initial plans for the fair — and won over the conservatives with his personal charm and enthusiasm. Later, unknown to him, however, they decided among themselves that their country and their individual reputations would be served best if they ignored the so-called "new" architecture and adhered strictly to a style they called "Roman classic."

Once the easterners had arrived in Chicago, Root worked tirelessly to ingratiate himself further and took great pains to see to their comfort. The night before the board of architects was to meet for the first time, Root gave an elaborate dinner party for the visitors. He saw to all the arrangements himself and directed the festivities, which lasted until late in the evening. Then, as his guests were departing, he insisted on seeing them to their separate coaches. It was bitter cold that January night, and Root was too busy looking after his guests to bother putting on a coat. Within a few hours he fell into bed exhausted, wracked by a fearsome chill. He was only forty-one, seven years older than Sullivan, but this illness was his last one. In four days he was dead of pneumonia.

The meetings went on without him, with Daniel Burnham offering words of welcome in his stead. Burnham had neither the talent nor the tenacity of jovial John Root, and he was quite obviously awed, presiding over a group that included some of architecture's most august figures. When the easterners advanced the notion that "Roman classic" should be the theme of the fair, Burnham readily agreed. He never paused to consider the possibility that innovative architecture of the moment might best express the life and character of modern America.

The easterners were a formidable group whom the Chicagoans were loath to oppose. Spokesman for the group was Richard Morris Hunt, who like Richardson and Sullivan had studied at the Beaux Arts in Paris. Hunt was a venerated leader whose word was law. So, one by one, Louis saw the ideas he had shared with Root being disregarded. Instead of a dynamic arrangement of structures, an exciting assortment of architectural themes and a rich use of color, the board decided that the major buildings should be restricted to a single style, built to the same height and scale, and all painted white. Those personally designed by the board members — the Administration Building, the Electricity Building and Machinery Hall, among others — were to be arranged symmetrically into a Court of Honor that surrounded a large central

The Fair's Court of Honor was described as "Roman classic" by conservative architects and "Roman imitation" by critics.

The broad basins and shimmering lagoons were among the only elements of the Chicago Fair to be given unanimous praise.

basin. "The emphasis will be on beauty," Hunt declared, and the others concurred.

Louis sat open-mouthed, too stunned at first to speak. In his mind's eye he could see that the World's Columbian Exposition was to be contained in a series of buildings as artificial as stage sets. From his standpoint the plan to which everyone had agreed was a sellout, a blight on the architectural face of America and an affront to the memory of John Root.

"Your plan will absolutely stifle the American spirit," he declared finally. "This 'Roman classic' you have chosen is a gross imitation, unworthy of an event that is supposed to glorify progress and achievement. It will suggest to the rest of the world that America is aesthetically stagnant, completely barren of new ideas." Louis pleaded vigorously, but he pleaded alone and spoke out in vain. The only response he received from his fellow architects was the assignment of a site for his Transportation Building that was outside the planned Court of Honor.

The location suited Louis, however. He felt confident that his design would make the building seem every bit as prominent as buildings in the Court of Honor. He was resolved to create something with a style and character all its own, even though he felt obliged to conform to proportions agreed on by the board. However, he did not feel obliged to make the Transportation Building white like the others. He thought it dishonest to try to delude fair-

Though the Transportation Building was not universally liked, it was the most original and ambitious structure at the Fair.

goers into thinking a building was made of white marble when in truth it was only a temporary structure with thin plaster walls.

Louis had decided that the Transportation Building should not look like a Roman temple but like what it was: an exposition hall filled with exhibits. Louis enlivened its facade with ornament and a bold use of color that pointed up what he envisioned as a monumental gateway to adventure — a great Golden Doorway flanked by arches.

The Transportation Building was 960 feet long and 256 feet wide, and it contained nearly two acres of floor space. Before it lay a reflecting pool in whose shimmering surface could be seen the brilliant reds, blues, yellows, oranges and greens of the walls, and the Golden Doorway, gleaming in the sun. The building's rainbow colors, its sculpture and bas relief, gave it a dazzling appearance, but the Golden Doorway stood out from everything else. It was a majestic piece of design, but for years critics have argued whether it related at all to the building's overall plan. Its dominance could never be denied, however.

The doorway was 100 feet long and 70 feet high, including its massive ornamented cornice. There were five concentric arches, one recessed within the other, that created a funnel-like effect to draw fairgoers inside to see the exhibits. There Louis had provided the appropriate setting for every imaginable kind of transport, from the Conestoga wagon to the balloon. There were stagecoaches, locomotives, baby carriages, Pullman cars in all their opulence and even a cageful of carrier pigeons. Inside and out, the Transportation Building captured the fancy of fairgoers. The classic grandeur of the Court of Honor may have awed them, but the Sullivan building seemed just what an exhibit hall should be.

The World's Columbian Exposition opened in May 1893 and lasted six months. Then the buildings were torn down, and Jackson Park returned to being swampland. Daniel Burnham boasted that the impact of the fair would inspire architects all over America to turn for stylistic guidance to the purity of the classics. And Louis Sullivan snorted that the damage to American archi-

Sullivan's Golden Doorway displayed a Moorish influence — in contrast to the prevalent Roman style of Fair architecture.

tecture done by the fair would not be repaired for at least fifty years.

Each man's predictions proved correct, as it happened, for one result of the fair was to give greater emphasis to the design approach of the traditionalists and to downgrade the Chicago School. Architecture, Louis Sullivan baldly stated, was dead in the United States, felled like a sapling to which cumbersome artificial limbs had been grafted.

Louis was a purist, unyielding and perhaps unreasonable, for even with the board of architects squarely behind him, the task of creating the kind of exposition he envisioned could not have been completed in time to meet the deadline. The "White City" by the lake may well have been a stuffy compromise, but it had an architectural unity that few people found displeasing. And, though far-seeing men like Sullivan denounced it, the "White City" alone was not responsible for the Chicago School's decline.

The year of the fair was also the year of another major business reversal, the panic of 1893, and this put a crimp in building activities until the end of the century. By then, however, popular tastes prevailed, and building design was frozen into a set of generally accepted styles: Roman for banks and railway stations, Old English for colleges and apartment houses, Gothic for churches. As far as Louis was concerned, it was all imported merchandise and all of it was bad.

The Transportation Building at the World's Columbian Exposition was far from Louis Sullivan's finest work, but partly because of the panic, it represented a turning point in the partnership of Adler & Sullivan and in Louis's life as well. In the two years before the panic, the firm had completed twenty buildings; in the two years following the panic only two commissions were finished. One of these, the Guaranty Building in Buffalo — renamed the Prudential Building in 1899 — turned out to be one of Sullivan's most lauded designs. It was also the last building he and Adler worked on together.

Though slightly taller, the fourteen-story Guaranty Building was very much like the earlier Wainwright Building in structure and appearance. Each was built around a court so that more offices would have windows. Each had soaring, uninterrupted piers, recessed spandrels and a series of round windows at the top-floor level. The most obvious difference between the two was that the entire exterior of the Guaranty Building, not just the spandrels, was sheathed in warm red terra-cotta and given Sullivan's characteristic embellishments. Just as Richardson before him had favored rough-surfaced granite, Sullivan had become a master at handling terra-cotta. This material was essentially burned clay — and never so splendidly modeled as when applied to a Sullivan design. His use of terra-cotta provided a whole new catalog of ornament, all of which seemed fussy and superfluous to his critics, but to his adherents was praiseworthy.

The Guaranty Building, completed in 1895 and still standing, was the finest expression of Sullivan's skyscraper philosophy. Its simple vertical form was nobly offset by ornamental detail. And it sparkled in warm terra cotta red at a time when most buildings were either gray or white. Inside the foyer (above) mosaic tile and marble paneling glowed in rich, contrasting colors; elevator cages and stairways were thick with sculpted ironwork (below).

The exterior facing of the Guaranty Building was not its only ornamented aspect. The lobbies and stairways inside the building were sumptuously decorated. The floors were mosaic tile, the walls marble-paneled, and the elevator grilles and stair rails were iron filigree. Lighting fixtures were recessed into circular ceiling panels on which leaf and petal designs appeared. This was Sullivan's most elaborate interior design, but it did not bring new clients to his door.

By the time the Guaranty Building opened in 1895, the depression produced by the panic of 1893 had completely crippled the building industry. Architects had run out of commissions, and many of them had quietly gone out of business. The fact that Adler & Sullivan maintained one of the largest offices in Chicago did not insulate it from the depression's dreary effects. With its staff of more than fifty draftsmen, designers and engineers, the firm had to find enough work to keep its people busy or it could not meet its payroll. And business was getting progressively worse.

Frank Lloyd Wright, a key member of the staff and one of the most loyal employees, was personally feeling the economic pinch. He was married by then, with two children and a house that was not yet paid for. Adler & Sullivan had generously advanced him money to buy the house, retaining its deed until the debt was repaid. But other creditors were closing in on him as the depression dragged on. To keep himself solvent, Wright had agreed to design a few houses on his own, outside the office. When Sullivan learned of these activities, he summoned Wright to his desk and raged at him: "You are contracted to work strictly for me. How *dare* you accept clients!"

"They are not 'clients,' Mr. Sullivan," Wright explained. "They're just friends, willing to pay me small sums to have small jobs done. And the money comes in handy in times like these, as I'm sure you understand."

"I understand only that this represents a division of interest," Sullivan said coldly, "and that you must end it at once."

"Mr. Sullivan, nothing I do on my own affects the work I do for you," Wright pleaded.

"Nonsense," said Sullivan. "Anything a man undertakes affects his work. I will not tolerate *division*."

"The few jobs I've taken have enabled me to keep paying bills at the same time I've repaid you and Mr. Adler what I owe on my home," Wright insisted.

"By violating your contract you are merely stealing from me at the same time you are repaying me," Sullivan said angrily. "I shall not issue the deed on your house until I have your assurance that this outside activity will cease."

Wright was angry too by then, for he felt he had worked hard to repay his debt. "Unless that deed is turned over to me at once," Wright said slowly, "I shall consider my contract terminated." Sullivan glanced away imperiously, as though Wright were no longer addressing him, and after a moment the young foreman stormed out of the office.

The issue did not end there, for Wright appealed to Adler, who favored any action that would put an end to the dispute. But Sullivan would hear none of it and was annoyed to think that Wright would go over his head to Adler. The subject did not come up again, though it continued to rankle beneath the surface. Eventually Adler sent the deed to Wright, who by then had quit the firm and gone out on his own.

Wright was not the only one to leave Adler & Sullivan. Other men were being asked to go, because there was so little work. Despite its fifteen-year existence, the firm lacked the capital reserve to weather the depression intact. Even so, Louis somehow managed to live as grandly when business was bad as when it was good. But Adler worried about the family that depended on him for support. One day he proposed as a stopgap — for himself and for the firm — that two more employees be let go and his own sons, Sidney and Abraham, be hired in their place. Although Abraham had studied engineering and Louis had always been fond of both boys, the idea was rejected. "I cannot sacrifice the experience and loyalty of anyone on the staff just for the sake of economy," said Louis.

"But think of *me,* Louis," said Adler. "Think of the sacrifice *I* might have to make, just for the sake of economy. Unless I can figure out some way to provide more for my family, I'll have to find something else to do. I may have to leave the company."

Sullivan looked at his partner with unconcealed scorn. "That would be worse than disloyalty," he said. "That would be treason."

"You leave me no choice," said Adler, but Louis had nothing further to say.

In July 1895 the president of the Crane Elevator Company offered Adler a long-term contract as a consulting engineer and general sales manager. The offer assured Adler a yearly salary greater than he had ever earned as an architect, but accepting it meant that he would end his partnership with Sullivan and turn his back on his profession. He did not want to do either, but the offer was too good to reject. He left Sullivan the suite of offices in the auditorium tower, where the staff — and the number of commissions — was dwindling week by week.

Sullivan refused to find himself a new partner and scoffed at suggestions that he join another firm. He felt secure in his own sense of eminence, and certain his business would thrive again once the economy had righted itself. If he ever realized it, he never acknowledged how valuable Dankmar Adler had been to him through the years. It was Adler who had dealt face to face with most of the clients; it was Adler who had sold Sullivan's ideas to them and persuaded the more unyielding ones that Sullivan's ideas were right. Louis tended to be arrogant when meeting a client's resistance. He was more likely to roll up his building plans and walk away than to discuss a single element of his design or even consider a compromise. He might well have supplied the creative energy that had kept Adler & Sullivan moving forward, but if so, Adler had been the pilot, the man who had steered the organization along. Now there was no one at the helm, and the firm was becalmed.

Adler's tenure with the Crane company lasted only six months. It ended by mutual consent then, for Adler did not like the business. He was quick to indicate to friends and former associates that he wanted to return to architecture, and though word of this was passed to Sullivan, Louis remained silent. He would not forgive Adler's "treason" under any circumstances. He made no gestures of amnesty toward his former partner, and Adler avoided him as much as possible.

Adler opened a small office on the sixth floor of the Auditorium Building, with his two sons acting as assistants. It was inevitable that he and Sullivan should meet accidentally in the lobby or in an elevator. When they did, they spoke to one another civilly, but with little warmth. Adler could not help feeling bitter toward his former junior partner, for the infrequent commissions he now received did little to restore him to the glory he had once enjoyed. However, though his commissions were few, they were more in number than Sullivan was receiving.

Louis could justifiably attribute his financial troubles to the lingering depression, but his situation did not improve when the depression ended. It was quickly forgotten — and would not be recalled for many years — that Sullivan's Transportation Building, with its imposing Golden Doorway, had been the only original work at the 1893 world's fair. Retaining his lavish quarters in the auditorium tower high above the city he loved, Louis seemed unaware that he had entered a period of virtual isolation. The men who had been closest to him — his brother, his partner and his most trusted assistant — were no longer with him. And the Golden Doorway, once a beckoning symbol of progress, had turned out to be a portal leading nowhere.

IX

THE YEARS WITH MARGARET

THE HOUSE Louis designed for his mother was the only dwelling in Chicago he ever occupied with any feeling of permanence. Before he lived there and after moving away, the places he called home were a succession of residences to which he felt little attachment. After leaving the house on Lake Park Avenue to his brother's family, Louis rented a place on the same street and in the same block where Albert had formerly lived. It was a large frame house, roomy enough to suit Louis's needs and to accommodate his vast collection of curios, mementos and books. But he did not plan to stay there long. It was merely a haven, a temporary resting place he would occupy until, hopefully, he could build or buy something better.

Although it was not a home for which he had any fondness, the house on Kimbark Avenue became his retreat. He had begun to write, trying to communicate his ideas on design and ornament to readers of architectural magazines. This activity increased after his partnership with Adler was dissolved — so much so that there were times when he literally sealed himself inside his house. He had to be alone to think, he insisted, to plan his articles, to refine his prose. But those closest to him, the remaining members of his staff, knew that he had become a heavy drinker and that he preferred drinking alone.

Sullivan's staff during his later years as an architect was made up mostly of young men, men right out of school or still apprenticing — men who understood Sullivan's theories, had similar convictions and were willing to be molded and directed by him. He had mellowed since Frank Lloyd Wright had come to him as a fledgling architect. He was not so high-strung as he had been, but he was still extremely demanding, and only those young men who respected his ability could tolerate his princely attitude.

For Sullivan there were specific advantages to employing young men. For one thing, they could be trained to adopt *his* approach to architectural problem-solving almost as second nature. For another, they would work for little money. He no longer had the financial wherewithal to maintain an experienced staff.

His young men certainly worked hard for him, whenever there was work to do. They wanted to please him, for to receive his approval indicated that they were making progress toward professional goals of their own. They were awed by his vigor and determination, kept alert by his precision and scrupulous attention to detail, but they had no emotional attachment to him. Sullivan was to his staff as Moses Woolson had been to him as a high school student years before. His cold, abrupt manner did not invite their affection. But they shared his hopes, his failures and his triumphs — and were particularly overjoyed when in 1897, an otherwise lean year, he received an unexpected commission in a most unlikely place, New York City.

New York had long been the citadel of the classical imitators, the eastern architects whose taste and influence had dominated the 1893 Chicago fair. Sullivan had never liked New York or felt at all welcome there, but a chance to contribute a building to that city's architectural landscape was not one he would have wanted to miss.

The client, a man named Bayard, after whom the building was named, had purchased a site on Bleecker Street, not far from the elegant residences surrounding Washington Square. The site was not large, but its narrowness posed no problem to Sullivan. He envisioned a slender twelve-story terra-cotta tower whose proportions would be emphasized by unbroken piers rising to an ornamented cornice. The approach was not a new one for Sullivan,

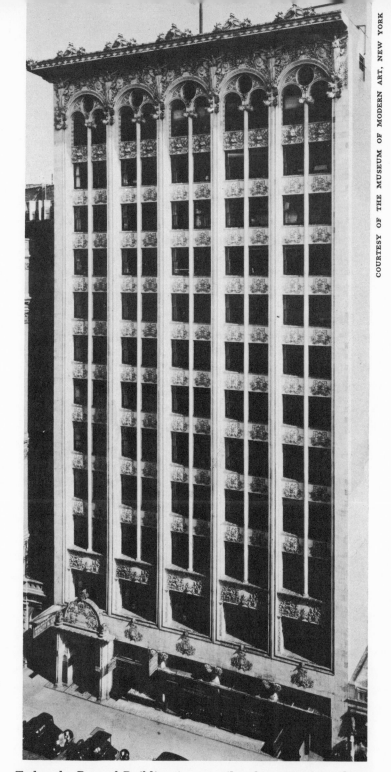

Today the Bayard Building is a mutilated masterpiece. Some time after this picture was taken, the facade was altered in a disastrous attempt to "modernize" the ground floor exterior.

but he made one notable variation. Alternating between the main piers, on each outside wall, were thin *mullions* — uprights dividing the windows — that rose in continuous lines. The piers and mullions were parallel all the way to the top floor. There the piers bent together to form large arches, and the mullions each split into delicate inner arches — above which there were circular windows, similar to those used on the Wainwright and Guaranty buildings.

The Bayard Building won considerable praise for Sullivan in the architectural journals. One writer went so far as to state that, at least in New York, this building represented the most successful attempt to date to solve the problem of the skyscraper. It brought the architect no new commissions, however, and remained his only structure in New York.

In 1898, about the time the Bayard Building was being finished, Louis abandoned the house on Kimbark Avenue and took a suite at a residential hotel called the Windermere. His apartment was smaller than the house had been, but it was less of a bother to maintain, while affording him the privacy he required. The rent was cheaper, too, a factor he had reason enough to consider. Ironically the Windermere faced one end of Jackson Park, offering a view of the razed site of his once much talked-of and now nearly forgotten Transportation Building.

Among the handful of commissions that occupied his time and tapped the facilities of his office in the closing years of the century was a plan to enlarge the Schlesinger & Mayer department store, which stood at State and Madison streets, Chicago's busiest corner. The store management had first contemplated expansion in 1891 and had discussed it with Adler and Sullivan, but for some reason the project had remained in abeyance. When it was finally activated, the two architects were no longer partners, and it was to Sullivan rather than Adler that the owners turned.

Sullivan was engaged to build a nine-story addition that would extend some sixty feet along the Madison Street side of the store. It seemed likely that he would follow a familiar course in designing this building, giving it the illusion of great height and vertical thrust by his treatment of the piers. But he did not; he emphasized the horizontal.

It was a marked change of approach for Sullivan — not a whim of design but the solution to a specific functional requirement. Each floor of the building was to have large open spaces where merchandise would be displayed and sold. The store owners wanted the maximum amount of daylight to reach these areas, so Sullivan made the windows as tall and wide as possible, within the limits set by structural steel. He used no vertical mullions, for they would have divided the windows and made them smaller. Since the horizontal areas between the tall steel columns were greater than the space between floor and ceiling beams, the windows ended up being wider than they were tall. To give unity to his design, Sullivan made the horizontal lines continuous — and subordinated the vertical lines by interrupting them with bands of ornament at each floor.

The outside of the building, faced in terra-cotta, was given Sullivan's scroll-like embellishments. The most noteworthy enhancement, and the one that was subject to long-lasting debate, was the ornamental iron casing applied to the building's two-story base. Designed to create a rich textured frame for each of the store's display windows, this half-inch iron coating was encrusted with flowers, vines, leaves and clusters of berries. Painstakingly executed from plaster molds made from pencil drawings, Schlesinger & Mayer's iron ornament was considered by some a virtuoso example of how technology and craft could be combined to achieve art. But many observers found the effect overpowering.

The store management was pleased with Sullivan's work, however. Though the new addition was not unanimously liked, it was universally talked about, which proved to be good for business. Later Sullivan was called on to design Schlesinger & Mayer's new main unit, which was to curve around the famous street corner and extend 150 feet south along State Street. Demolition of the two old buildings that had occupied this site was completed in

Detail of the iron ornament over the store's main entrance

The Carson, Pirie, Scott store (formerly Schlesinger & Mayer) still occupies the busiest street corner in downtown Chicago.

1902, and during the next two years Sullivan's design took shape in their place, adjoining the addition he had previously done.

Sullivan's second unit was three stories higher than the first, but it continued and extended the horizontal treatment he had begun. This building, with its gleaming, sculpted ironwork, was the center of interest long before the store had opened. But even before the building was finished, the store was sold, and Schlesinger & Mayer became Carson, Pirie, Scott & Company. The new owners awarded the commission for a third new unit to Sullivan's old opponent Daniel Burnham when further expansion was called

for in 1906. The timing of this rebuff made it all the more dis-
heartening, for the years between commissions for the first unit
of the store and the last had seasoned Louis's personal life with
the most remarkable mixture of joy and sadness he had ever
known.

In 1899, while striding briskly up Madison Street one day, he
had come upon a handsome young woman walking her dog. He
had stooped to pet the dog as the three of them approached an
intersection, but he had really been more struck by the owner
than the animal. The woman was tall and striking, with dark
brown hair and deep brown eyes. Louis spoke to her and she
smiled, undismayed by his boldness. He said he was too busy at
the moment to see her to her door but would like very much to see
her at another time, whenever it was mutually convenient. She
told him where she lived and invited him to visit her, and soon he
did — many times.

Her name was Margaret Hattabough, and she was twenty-
seven. She had been married once, but not happily, and she
seemed receptive to the idea of marrying again. On July 1, 1899,
she became Louis Sullivan's wife. Their fifteen-year age difference was of as little concern to Louis as it was to Margaret, for he
was following a pattern set by his father and brother.

Later that year Margaret had her first view of Ocean Springs
and of Louis's cottage surrounded by azalea and palmetto bushes,
dogwoods, wild honeysuckle and his immaculately kept rose
garden. It was Louis's special joy each day to select one perfect
rose, a blossom as extravagantly shaped by nature as the orna-
ments he fashioned in terra-cotta, and to present it to Margaret on
a two-foot stem. She gloried in the attention he lavished on her,
and he rejoiced now in having someone with whom to share his
pleasures.

The months in Ocean Springs, a kind of delayed honeymoon,
were relaxing and enjoyable. Louis and Margaret were busy much
of the time, pruning and puttering in the garden, adding decorative touches to the cottage, taking long walks along the path by

the bay. They also found time for simply doing nothing, for indulging in that blissful idleness that must be cherished because it must so quickly end. When winter winds began to rattle the limbs of the live oak trees, the Sullivans left their castle in the wilderness and returned to Louis's rooms in the Windermere. The honeymoon was over.

Back at his desk in the auditorium tower, Louis followed up on the few commissions that had come into the office at the time he first began work on Schlesinger & Mayer. But there were no *new* projects, nothing fresh to challenge his creative mettle. He answered his mail, talked with his staff and then turned his energy full force on writing.

In June 1900 he read a paper he had written, "The Young Man in Architecture," before a Chicago meeting of the Architectural League. In it he lashed out at his fellow architects and denounced contemporary building design as the offspring of an illegitimate marriage between assorted mongrel styles of the past. Then, addressing himself to the future, he called on young architects to rebel against accepted form and, most of all, to demand the freedom to be individual. His bitterness was great, and it was easy to understand, for the classical imitators he loathed were winning profitable commissions and he was getting none.

Continuing his one-man campaign for recognition, he convinced the editor of a weekly magazine, *The Interstate Architect and Builder*, to let him write a series of articles on American architecture. The articles, all interrelated, were composed as a series of imaginary dialogues between the author and a student who had just graduated from a school of architecture. The young man asked questions, and Sullivan answered them — loftily, pontifically, often scornfully. Conceived as a kind of kindergarten of the mind for young men seeking careers in architecture, the articles were referred to by their author as *Kindergarten Chats*. Wordy, repetitive, at times eloquent, at other times clumsy — especially when Sullivan injected his own poetry — the *Chats* became his testament. Through fifty-two articles he spun out his passion and his contempt for what he felt American architecture had lost by not pursuing the course he himself had pioneered.

Sullivan used the *Kindergarten Chats* as a platform for mounting attacks on the advocates of tradition, foremost among whom were professors in schools of architecture. To him these institutions were harmful and undemocratic; they did not teach architecture, only a mindless acceptance of rules. He was equally vehement when discussing the trend in architecture that encouraged architects to design banks as Roman imitations. Perhaps the banker should be made to wear a toga and conduct his transactions in Latin, Sullivan suggested.

Some of his comparisons were exaggerated to the point of absurdity, and much of his scorn obviously resulted from resentment. But as a total work, despite these flaws, *Kindergarten Chats* succeeded brilliantly in expressing the many facets of an architect's point of view. It was the first work of its kind to treat architecture as one of many strains of intellectual thought — and to consider the architect in the same realm as the poet, the philosopher and the artist. An architect, wrote Sullivan, is the interpreter of his time. He is a poet who uses building materials instead of words for self-expression. To Sullivan a knowledge of craft was but one requirement an architect had to meet. Common sense, a disciplined mind, a humane character and, of course, an extraordinary gift of expression were even more important.

Writing *Kindergarten Chats* was an all-absorbing job that took Louis more than a year. He hurled himself into the task with customary vigor, committing to paper the thoughts and opinions he had stored inside for years. But the series was no substitute for commissions, as little money would be earned from the effort. Louis and Margaret were finally compelled to move out of the Windermere and into the smaller, seedier Virginia "hotel apartments," about a mile from the Auditorium Building.

Hotel life did not suit either of them. They felt cramped and frankly miserable at the Virginia. Fortunately there was the cottage at Ocean Springs to retreat to every autumn. It was there

Louis and Margaret pose in their garden at Ocean Springs.

that Louis completed all but one of the *Kindergarten Chats* late in 1901. He and Margaret celebrated Christmas together and toasted the new year. Then, leaving her behind to enjoy a few weeks' additional rest, Louis returned to Chicago to finish the last of his *Chats* and begin work on whatever new commissions might have come into the office during his absence.

But there was nothing, and though Louis wrote optimistically to former associates that business had begun picking up, he knew there was no reason to feel hopeful about his prospects. The fault, he assumed, lay in the fact that people were not being educated well enough to appreciate him. He could not imagine that he himself was at least partly to blame for the lack of work.

First of all, word of his explosive temper — and of his drinking — had tarnished his image. Secondly, his office no longer had the facilities or the staff in depth it had possessed when he and Adler were partners. Louis was like a midget competing among giants, and commissions would be harder than ever to win. He wanted to keep busy, but not even his papers and speeches could create a renewal of interest in his work.

He was happiest at Ocean Springs, caring for his roses, free from anxieties resulting from his steeply declining career. He and Margaret shared a tranquil existence in Mississippi, but each time they returned to Chicago their situation grew worse and worse.

In the summer of 1905 the Sullivans moved out of the Virginia and into a still cheaper flat in the Lessing Annex, a few blocks away. People now became aware how much Sullivan had aged in recent years. His face was heavily lined, his complexion coarse, and his eyes were swollen from weariness. He was still consuming great quantities of coffee to remain alert, but he was also drinking great quantities of alcohol. His nights were wakeful, his days at times a blur. No wonder potential clients did not seek his services. Yet when an occasional commission did come in, he was the stern and sober uncompromising architect of old.

At his office, when there was no work to do, Louis whiled away the hours chatting with the men who remained on his staff. He would talk at length about practically anything, and they would obediently listen. Sometimes, when seated at his desk, he would gaze for hours at the misty blue waters of Lake Michigan beyond his window, or study the photographic plates he had made of his roses at Ocean Springs. The few opportunities he had for an article to be published gave him the impetus to work with furious energy. And when he had finished an essay, he delighted in reading it aloud to his staff. These were his best moments, moments when his enthusiasm and unsuppressed glee at being able to attack his "enemies" lifted his spirits above their normal gloom. At other times he was largely pathetic, and no more so than to his wife.

Life had grown dismal for Margaret, who had been accustomed to being waited on, deferred to and dominated by her husband. Now it was she who had to be the assertive one, straining to bend Louis's iron will to her own. This was made all the more difficult by the fact that when Louis drank he was unapproachable — a quiet, sullen recluse withdrawn into a world whose landscape was shaped by his own delusion.

It became increasingly obvious, if only to Margaret, that Louis's earnings and meager savings were not sufficient to support the two of them. Yet she could not even think of taking a job because of the need to look after her husband. Besides, she knew he would never permit it. She worried about him when he was at the office and fretted over him while he was home, where he was either surly or uncommunicative. She usually had to help him into bed at night, and there were times when he was in such a stupor that she had to summon a member of the hotel staff or another resident for assistance.

The untroubled life at Ocean Springs was becoming a luxury they could not afford, yet that was the only place where Louis was at peace with himself or with Margaret. And when he was not at peace, he was impossible. It became clear to Margaret that her husband's years of glory had irredeemably passed and he would never regain the esteem or the prominence he had once known.

But, she reasoned, she herself was still young; she had not given up. She could work, she could earn a living, and perhaps someday she might become a novelist — which she had wanted to be for a long time. But she knew she could not achieve anything while married to Louis Sullivan. She could not save him; she could only hope to save herself. She had no choice but to turn her back on the man with whom she had lived for seven years. Though divorce proceedings were withheld until 1917, the Sullivans were separated in 1906 — permanently.

X

LOUIS ALONE

IN THE FIRST YEARS of the twentieth century, America experienced a renewal of the surge toward urbanization that had been under way intermittently since the Civil War. At the time Louis Sullivan had first become Dankmar Adler's partner, little more than a fourth of the population lived in cities. By 1910 the percentage had increased to nearly half. In Chicago there had been so much commercial construction that the lakefront was rimmed with an almost solid wall of buildings. And in New York, where skyscrapers were reaching greater and greater heights, the Singer Building soared forty-seven stories over the Manhattan skyline. The Woolworth Building would exceed it by thirteen stories in 1913 and remain the world's tallest edifice for nearly two decades.

For Louis Sullivan, ironically, the skyscraper period ended early in the twentieth century. The career of the man who had given form and distinction to the tall office building was stagnating. He was still working now and then, and his designs were still significant, but his efforts were on a less imposing scale.

In 1907 the officers of the National Farmers' Bank of Owatonna, Minnesota, announced that a long-needed new building would at last be erected. It had been in the planning stage for several years. The officers knew what its physical layout should be, and its approximate size as well, but they had been undecided as to its style. The so-called "classic" approach, with predominantly Roman elements, had been considered and rejected, because it was being used so widely and so badly in bank buildings then. The architects who had been consulted from time to time seemed content to follow traditional patterns and assemble proposed designs from well-thumbed architectural handbooks. But the officers of the Owatonna bank said no. They were strictly businessmen, but they had taste, and they wanted their new bank to be something special.

Owatonna was a farm town, sometimes called the butter capital of the world, because it lay in the heart of Minnesota dairy country. Even though it was situated some three hundred miles northeast of Chicago, the men who managed its National Farmers' Bank cast keen eyes at what was being done in that metropolis and at the work of the city's leading architects. They began to read architectural journals, hoping to discover a man with an individual approach, a man who might be capable of designing a bank that not only fulfilled practical needs but also possessed the warmth and informality that residents of a small midwestern town would find inviting. One of the bank's vice-presidents read an article by Louis Sullivan, published in *The Craftsman,* and found himself fascinated by what it said.

Written in Sullivan's customarily strong, passionate language, the piece denounced prevailing attitudes toward architecture as unworthy of a free people. Are all Americans hypocrites? Sullivan asked. Are they ashamed to be honest, afraid to be original? Are their souls without poetry? If not, he said, then current architectural standards are artificial and irrelevant, pointlessly chained to tradition.

The article was devastating, not at all likely to win friends for Louis among his generation of architects, many of whom by then were doing original, non-imitative work. But the Owatonna bankers were impressed. A man as forthright as Louis Sullivan, as unafraid to speak his mind, was the kind of man they had been seeking. They wrote, urging him to accept their small commission, and he, delighted to have found such appreciative readers and truly desperate for work, eagerly accepted.

The National Farmers' Bank is now Owatonna's Security Bank.

What Louis designed for Owatonna was a two-story structure made up of cubelike forms that were joined together as solidly as a strongbox. It was different from any of his houses or office buildings, different from practically anything he had ever designed. The only work to which it might be compared is the Transportation Building, for the bank's windows were arches which, though smaller, appeared no less massive than the fabled Golden Doorway, and it fairly gleamed with color.

The bank's exterior walls were of reddish brown sandstone and dark red brick. The front and side walls were trimmed with a bronze-green outer band and a glass mosaic inner band that was flecked with green, white and gold. Inside the bank there were black marble counters, bronze grilles, green tile floors and red brick walls. There were colorful murals and leaded-glass windows tinted with green and violet panels, through which generous amounts of sunlight poured.

That National Farmers' Bank was the first of seven "strongbox" banks that Sullivan would design in such towns as Algona, Iowa; Sidney, Ohio; and Columbus, Wisconsin. Although he produced a variety of houses, stores and even a church during his last years in practice, his midwestern banks, with their strong colors and gracious interiors, were his most winning efforts.

[144]

Sullivan's handiwork is apparent in the tellers' cage design (above) and in interior ornament over the doorway (below).

His commissions were inevitably smaller now, because he had no engineering talent on his staff and only a few draftsmen to assist him. His income was so meager that by the end of 1908 he knew he could no longer maintain his cottage at Ocean Springs. In fact, he could not even afford a railroad ticket to get there. He sold the little house with everything in it, for he could not bring himself to visit the place once it was sold — not even to remove the belongings he had left behind. Later he also gave up his art collection. These items had always been worth more to him in memories than in money, but now the money had become more important. He put everything up for auction late in November 1909 — the Oriental rugs, the Chinese and Japanese vases, the bronze and jade carvings, the paintings and even the books.

The proceeds from the auction, and those from the sale of his cottage, paid Louis's debts and allowed him to live awhile without worry. But eventually that money, too, ran out, and Louis had to strip away what few comforts and niceties of life remained to him. In December 1910 he was compelled to resign from the Chicago Club, whose membership he had distinguished for twenty years. Happily, the Cliff Dwellers, an equally proud but somewhat more compassionate club nearby, lent a hand and made him an honorary member.

The following year Louis had to abandon his apartment in Lessing Annex and move into two tiny rooms in the rundown Warner Hotel. It was close to Lake Michigan, and Louis liked living near the water, but it was certainly a dismal place to be. He looked on it as a temporary retreat, as he had the other suites and apartments he had occupied, but the Warner Hotel was destined to be his home for the rest of his life.

He was poor, and he was generally neglected, but he was not entirely forgotten. Though few clients were making demands on his time, there were critics who praised his "strongbox" banks, and there were students and interested professionals who gathered in goodly numbers whenever he lectured. He was a prophet

Frank Lloyd Wright posed for this portrait a few years before he renewed his friendship with Louis.

of change who had been largely unheeded, so it soothed his ego to know he could still command an audience.

After one of his lectures in 1914 he was approached by a man who seemed a total stranger, except that his face had a vaguely familiar look. The man smiled, and Louis was suddenly sure he had known this person long ago. "Mr. Sullivan," the man said, and now the voice was unmistakable.

"Mr. Wright," Louis replied, extending his hand. The two men greeted each other warmly and spoke of the "old days" without a trace of rancor. But Frank Lloyd Wright could not suppress a pang of sorrow. His image of his former employer was shattered, for the once-vigorous Sullivan looked drawn and bent. Some days later Wright visited Louis's office, only to be saddened by its din-

Wright pioneered "prairie architecture," which was tailored to the Midwest's flat open spaces. Like Evans House, built in Chicago in 1908, these homes stressed a horizontal theme.

The Larkin Building, Buffalo, had plain brick walls, inside and out, but the focus of Wright's design was a sunny, sky-lit interior. The building, erected in 1904, has been razed.

giness and the pall of inactivity that seemed to hang heavily within. Louis's desk was dusty and unkempt, littered with papers and photographs that were cracked and curled from age. To Wright, Louis seemed a man shorn of spirit, lacking the streak of arrogance that had always fended off failure and counteracted whatever reverses he had suffered. There were shades of humor in Louis's conversation, some of the old salty bravado, but little of the dynamic energy that Wright remembered.

The two men talked long and earnestly, and they shook hands with great affection when they parted. Louis was not one to forgive easily or express the depth of his feelings, but his reunion with Wright was like a tonic. Knowing this, Wright returned often to Louis's office, and to his bedside during his painful last years.

By 1918 the last of Louis's youthful staff had left him. Even the office boy had found more favorable surroundings. Louis was completely alone now and nearly penniless. "For me the future is a blank," he wrote one of his former draftsmen, and things did not improve. In a short time he was forced to move out of the auditorium tower. He had worked there in a kind of sanctum for twenty-seven years, but now he could no longer afford it. The owners of the building offered him two small rooms on the second floor. These were assuredly dingy quarters, but the rent was nominal, and Louis gratefully accepted the offer. By 1920, however, he could not even afford this office, and with reluctance and an aching sense of failure he moved to a cheaper address on Prairie Avenue, some blocks away. It was twenty minutes by foot from his rooms at the Warner Hotel, which cost him a sorry nine dollars a week.

At this stage of his life, neither his home nor his office held much attraction for him. On days when the weather was good, he generally sought a bench in a park near the Warner. On poor days he sat by a fire in the Cliff Dwellers Club, where he was always welcome. Small comforts pleased him, and he found joy in the impromptu meetings with old associates, men with whom he

Sullivan used this portrait as a Christmas greeting in 1920.

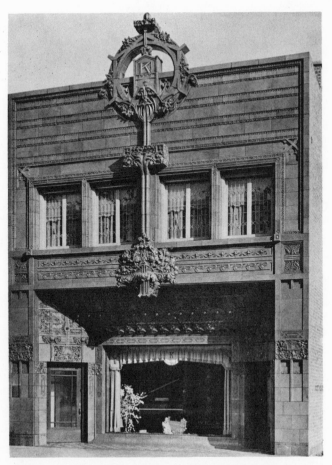

The building that housed Krause Music Store on Lincoln Avenue was eventually turned into an undertaking establishment.

could share a few moments' conversation and exchange ideas and opinions on architecture.

In 1921 he was asked to work on a small music store to be built on Lincoln Avenue. The store was to occupy the ground floor, above which the owner, William Krause, planned to live. Another architect had conceived the plan of the building and designed the interior. Sullivan's only contribution was the building's facade and store front, which he finished in dull green terra-cotta panels to set off a huge, recessed, picture-frame show window. It was a minor contribution at best, but it represented the last of the one hundred and twenty-six buildings he had worked on as an architect.

That same year George Nimmons and Max Dunning, two of Louis's fellow Cliff Dwellers who happened to be young architects, outlined a plan to him. They were aware how miserable he was when inactive, and they felt strongly that he still had much to contribute. They suggested, first, that he design a series of plates that would appear in a folio illustrating his theory of architectural ornament. Second and more important, they suggested that he write his autobiography. The two men said they would make sure his work was paid for and that both projects were published.

Louis was jubilant, of course, flattered that the architects had thought enough to make him such a proposal and eager to be busy again. In January 1922 he plunged into work on both projects, turning out masterful drawings at his office by day and writing portions of his autobiography at the Cliff Dwellers at night. Meanwhile, Dunning and Nimmons talked to other architects who belonged to the club and managed to raise some money to pay Louis an advance before his work was finished. Then they persuaded the editor of the *Journal of the American Institute of Architects* to publish the autobiography in monthly installments over the course of a year. Afterwards, they hoped, the A.I.A. would reprint the entire work in book form.

Louis devoted all of 1922 and much of 1923 to the two tasks at hand. The drawings demanded meticulous work, but the autobiography was more involving and even more time-consuming. Long before it was completed, though, Louis had composed its title, one that was every bit as original as *Kindergarten Chats* had been. He called it *The Autobiography of an Idea*.

It was an odd choice of title, but the work itself was an odd kind of autobiography. It was written in the third person. Sullivan never once referred to himself as "I," but always as "he." His approach was that of an intent biographer probing into the life of his subject, a man whose thoughts and feelings he happened to know extremely well. In addition, the autobiography was not wholly accurate and not really complete. Louis dwelt so long on his childhood and young manhood that he was two-thirds finished by the time his central character had departed for Paris at age eighteen. The autobiography ended with the World's Columbian Exposition of 1893, leaving the last thirty years of the architect's life for future historians to piece together.

Louis wrote of his parents, his grandparents, of George Tompson and John Edelmann, Dankmar Adler and Frank Lloyd Wright. But there was no mention of his brother Albert, or of Albert's wife, or of his own wife either. He wrote rapturously of his cottage at Ocean Springs and lamented that it had been destroyed by a "hurricane." He wrote only what he wanted his readers to believe, and the Louis Sullivan he described — brilliant, poetic, prophetic and in all ways wise — was the way he wished to be remembered.

The Autobiography of an Idea appeared serially in the *Journal* from June 1922 to August 1923, at which time the editors decided it should indeed become a book, and Louis revised much of it accordingly. By this time he had completed the twenty drawings that would make up the second promised volume, whose title, while more orthodox than the others, was also considerably longer: *A System of Architectural Ornament According with a Philosophy of Man's Powers.* The excellence of the drawings indicated that even at age sixty-six, with paralysis beginning to grip his right hand and arm, Sullivan could still produce the delicate lines and exquisite shapes for which he had once been famous.

His general health had begun to decline now. In addition to the paralysis that was gradually crippling him, his heart had become so swollen it literally bulged behind his ribs. Still he drank cup after cup of strong coffee. Fortunately his bouts with the liquor bottle occurred less often when he was busy, which was another reason his friends had been eager to have him engrossed in work again. He lived solely on their contributions, for the fees his writ-

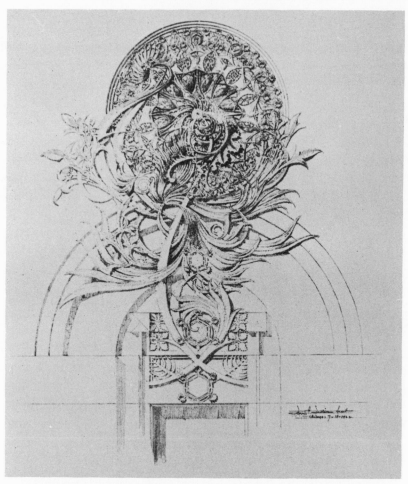

This flower petal-and-leaf design was one of the pencil drawings reproduced in *A System of Architectural Ornament,* Sullivan's second book, which he did not live to see published.

ings earned were very small. The men collected money to pay his
rent, took him to the theater and looked after him as if they were
his sons.

Frank Lloyd Wright visited him often, traveling to Chicago
from his Wisconsin estate. He came whenever he could, for there
was no doubt that Sullivan welcomed his visits. It grieved him
to see that Louis's life was ebbing, yet there was no doubt of
that either. Louis's eyes were bright, his mind was alert, but

where once he had walked with a swagger, he now clung tightly to Wright's arm when they went anywhere together. At street corners Louis would pause to catch his breath before descending from the curb to the pavement.

By January 1924 Louis had completed the introduction to his *System of Architectural Ornament.* He had also completed a piece in praise of Frank Lloyd Wright for *Architectural Record* magazine. It was the last article he would ever write, for he could no longer handle a pencil. By February he had grown so weak he was unable to leave his hotel room, and a nurse had to be with him at all times. Max Dunning and George Nimmons looked in on him almost daily, and he was always an agreeable host. He never complained about his health, only about the state of the country and the wretched state into which he felt architecture had fallen.

Dunning, sensing that Sullivan might have only a few weeks to live, telegraphed the A.I.A. Press and urged that single copies of both the *Autobiography* and *System of Architectural Ornament* be rushed to Chicago in time for Louis to see the final product of his labors. The A.I.A. could comply only in part to the request, for the latter book was still not ready. But that did not matter. Dunning remembered the look of joy that crossed Louis's face when he saw the first bound copy of his autobiography. He seemed renewed in spirit and reinvigorated despite his illness.

On April 11 Wright visited him again. How proud Louis was of his onetime junior draftsman, a man who was now America's foremost architect. Wright's office buildings, his churches, hotels and especially his houses — earth-colored, ground-hugging, richly unique symbols of a new life in the American West and Southwest — had earned him world renown. Sullivan extended his hand, his stronger left hand, and made a shaky attempt to climb out of bed. "No, you mustn't," Wright cautioned.

"Yes, I will," Sullivan insisted. He struggled toward the edge of the bed without assistance and then stopped, letting his feet dangle. Wright wrapped his own overcoat and muffler around the old man's wasted body and covered his feet with a blanket. Louis beamed warmly at Wright. "That book there," he said, pointing toward the autobiography, which sat on a table near his bed. "Hand it to me."

Wright did so, saying nothing but knowing full well what the book was. Sullivan took it and flipped it open. "Have you something to write with?" he asked. Wright fumbled briefly in his jacket pocket and produced a long yellow pencil. Sullivan took it with his left hand but could not raise his right arm or control his fingers well enough to make an inscription. "It doesn't matter," he said brightly, returning the book to Wright. "You were never sentimental."

By this time Wright could feel himself trembling. It was all he could do to hold back tears. Now Sullivan pointed to a sheaf of papers that leaned against a wall across the room. "Take them," he said. "I want them to be yours."

Flipping through the papers, Wright realized they were all that remained of Louis's drawings. Some of them dated back to Louis's years at the Beaux Arts in Paris. There were sketches he had made when he first joined Dankmar Adler, as well as designs for ornament and some of the finely drawn details of the various buildings he had designed. What Wright was being given was more than a memento; it was, in fact, a record of Louis's place in American architecture for all the years that he had been working.

Wright wanted to say something, but his voice failed him. Yet words could not have adequately expressed what he felt then, and looking at Sullivan he knew that words were not expected of him.

The old man seemed suddenly weary, so Wright removed the topcoat and muffler and helped him back beneath the covers. For a moment Louis lay motionless, his eyes shut tight. Wright put on his topcoat. He was about to tiptoe out of the room and signal the nurse to reenter, when he saw Sullivan smile and nod his head. "You, Frank . . . have had success where *I* have failed,"

This architectural study — the detail of a gilded plaster ornament designed for a Chicago theater building — was among the drawings Sullivan gave to Wright. It is dated May 6, 1884.

he said very softly. "In your work . . . I see what I have been talking about . . . all these years."

"You flatter me," said Wright. "I've done very little."

"You have done . . . what I could not do myself," said Sullivan. "It is *you* who have created the new architecture in America. But" — and now his voice rang with the firmness that Wright recalled from thirty years before — "I don't believe you could have done it . . . without *me*."

It was Wright's last visit. Three days later Louis Sullivan was dead. A modest funeral was held, and he was buried in a grave beside his parents in Chicago's Graceland Cemetery.

Louis was mourned by the men who had been closest to him, by the handful of critics in the United States and abroad who alone recognized his greatness, but by few others. It was only with the passing of time and the writing of history that he has begun to be appreciated and understood. His influence, his thinking and his philosophy have proved of more lasting significance than even his buildings, for many of these have been demolished and others are falling into decrepitude. Though his architecture is his monument, he has been memorialized since his death because of the sense of direction he tried to give architecture at a time when, like a wheezy locomotive, it was running out of steam.

Sullivan did not prescribe a style of design. He merely dictated a method of thought that, in the years since World War II, has finally been accepted and come to be applied. He did not turn his back on the past, as many detractors maintained, but he insisted that the past could not be imitated. If form was to be true to its function, he said, tradition would have to be adapted and restated to meet new and more demanding needs.

Sullivan is considered the father of the skyscraper, though he was not the first to design a tall office building. He is often called America's first modern architect, though it was Richardson before him who first stated a contemporary American theme. He is considered an architectural giant, though Wright emerged as the greater figure. And, though some scholars and critics have belittled his architecture, he is now assured a prominent place in architectural history.

If nothing else, Sullivan provided a bridge between Richardson and Wright. He applied modern technology to Richardson's individuality of design — out of which Wright created a bold, new and distinctly American style.

As the years passed, Frank Lloyd Wright developed a towering ego that allowed him to give quarter to absolutely no one, but he never forgot his teacher. Through a long and illustrious career that ended only with his death in 1959, he never failed to credit Sullivan for his success. In everything Wright said about architecture and in everything he wrote about his life, Sullivan was always referred to reverently as "the master."

GLOSSARY

ACOUSTICS: the science of sound; an auditorium is said to have good acoustics if the sound is transmitted evenly and if the sound is true.

ARCH: a curved element, supported at either end, that spans an opening — window, door or passageway.

ARCHITECTURE: the science and art of designing and constructing buildings; also, the product of building design and construction.

BEAM: a horizontal supporting member of a structural frame.

BEARING WALL: wall on which rests part of a building's structural load.

BRICK: a masonry unit, made of a baked clay mixture, that normally measures two inches by four inches by eight inches.

BROWNSTONE: a reddish brown sandstone used in construction.

CAST IRON: iron that has been shaped by being poured into a mold after being heated to a molten, or liquid, state.

CLAPBOARD: a plank used to cover many wood-frame buildings; it is applied in horizontal strips, the top edge thinner than the bottom so that the strips will overlap easily to weatherproof the building.

CLASSICAL: that which adheres to an established, and ancient, form or standard.

COLUMN: an upright unit on which weight rests; a supporting pillar.

CORNICE: a projecting and sometimes decorative band of trim at the top of a building wall.

CUPOLA: a small, domelike or towerlike structure rising from a rooftop.

DESIGN: the drawn plans from which a structure will be built.

[161]

DRAFTSMAN: one who makes sketches or designs of buildings to be constructed.

ENGINEERING: the techniques that make practical use of a pure science such as physics.

FACADE: the dominant side of a building, usually the front.

FILIGREE: ornamental work that is always delicate, sometimes fanciful.

FLY LOFT: the portion of a theater building that rises above the stage, the area into which scenery is raised.

FOUNDATION: the bottommost part of a structure; it rests in or on the supporting earth.

FRESCO: a wall painting; the pigment is applied while the plaster is still wet.

GOTHIC: the architecture of the thirteenth, fourteenth, and fifteenth centuries in Europe; it was rendered in stone and characterized in part by pointed arches.

GRANITE: a coarse-grained rock of great strength.

GRILLE: intersecting metal bars that form a decorative screen.

INGOT: a casting obtained when molten metal is poured into a mold before further shaping and processing has been determined.

LEADED GLASS: painted glass panels separated by narrow lead dividers.

MARBLE: limestone in a crystalline state, usually with a smooth, polished surface that is desirable in construction.

MASONRY: a type of construction that involves the application of brick, tile or stone that is held together and in place by mortar.

MASS: the size and bulk of an object.

MEDIEVAL: characteristic of the Middle Ages, which extended from the fifth to the fourteenth centuries in Europe.

MOSAIC: a decoration made of small pieces of stone or glass of different colors inlaid to form a pattern or design.

MULLION: an upright division between a series of window panels or doors.

ORNAMENTATION: detail that is molded, painted or added to a building for decorative purposes.

PIER: an upright unit that may be used by itself to help support a building or as part of a supporting wall.

PYRAMID: a masonry form possessing a square base and triangular sides that meet in a point at the top.

RAFTER: unit of support beneath the boarding that covers a roof.

RECESSED: that which is cut into the surface of a ceiling or wall.

ROMANESQUE: a style of architecture that originated in Europe in the Middle Ages and is based on ancient Roman forms.

SANDSTONE: a noncrystalline rock resembling sand particles that have been cemented together.

SCAFFOLD: a temporary structure that supports platforms aiding workmen in construction.

SCULPT: to work in three-dimensional forms, chiseling into stone or molding clay.

SETBACK: an indentation of the upper stories of a building to provide better ventilation and more sunlight.

SETTLEMENT: the gradual sinking of a building's foundation into earth too soft to resist its weight.

SHINGLES: wedge-shaped pieces of wood applied in overlapping layers to outside walls or roofs to keep out wind and rain.

SPANDREL: an exterior wall panel that extends horizontally between a building's vertical columns, from the sill of one window to the top of the window below it.

STEEL: iron combined with varying amounts of carbon for the varying degrees of hardness and elasticity needed in construction.

STYLE: a particular, distinctive or characteristic form of construction; it usually reflects a specific period in architectural history.

SUSPENSION BRIDGE: a bridge whose roadway is supported by cables hung between steel or masonry towers.

TECHNOLOGY: the sciences of the industrial arts; improved technology results in improved methods of building or manufacturing.

TERRA-COTTA: cast and baked units made of brownish orange earthenware, usually larger and more intricately molded than bricks.

TURRETS: small towers that protrude from the corners of a building and generally rise above it.

VERANDA: a long, partly enclosed porch that is attached to a house.

ACKNOWLEDGMENTS

THE AUTHOR wishes to express heartfelt appreciation for the research material and editorial counsel so graciously provided by John M. Dixon, A.I.A., Senior Editor, *Architectural Forum*. For generous assistance in supplying or locating illustrative material, the author is particularly indebted to: Mrs. Miriam L. Lesley, Head, Art Department, The Free Library of Philadelphia; Joseph W. Molitor and Richard Nickel, photographers; Richard C. Nylander, Curatorial Assistant, the Society for the Preservation of New England Antiquities; Mrs. Henry Ottmann, Research Assistant, Department of Architecture and Design, The Museum of Modern Art; Adolf K. Placzek, Librarian, Avery Architectural Library, Columbia University; Mrs. Mary Frances Rhymer, Curator of Prints, Chicago Historical Society; Miss Ruth E. Schoneman, Librarian, Ryerson and Burnham Libraries, The Art Institute of Chicago; and historian Edward Teitelman. The index was prepared by Bruce Macomber.

Below, listed by page number and position, are sources for all the pictures that appear in this book:

Courtesy of The Art Institute of Chicago: Frontispiece, 5 (bottom), 27, 66, 68, 95 (top), 97, 114, 115, 150.

Avery Architectural Library, Columbia University: 4, 5 (top left and top right), 40 (left), 108, 110, 111, 147, 157.

Society for the Preservation of New England Antiquities, Boston: 6, 19, 20.

Photographed by Michael Hampton: 21, 40 (right), 65 (top).

M.I.T. photo: 37.

ACKNOWLEDGMENTS

Courtesy of The Free Library of Philadelphia: 47 (both).

Courtesy of the Chicago Historical Society: 52 (both), 53, 71, 117 (both), 118, 120.

Courtesy of The Museum of Modern Art, New York: 65 (bottom), 76, 84 (both), 130, 148 (both).

Photographed by Richard Nickel: 74.

Chicago Architectural Photographing Company: 89, 95 (bottom), 99, 100, 106, 122, 123 (both), 134, 138, 144, 145 (both), 151.

Courtesy of Harry Weese & Associates, Chicago: 90 (both), 91 (both), all photographed by Richard Nickel.

Photographed by Richard L. Bliss, St. Louis chapter, A.I.A.: 104 (both).

From *The Idea of Louis Sullivan* by John Szarkowski, University of Minnesota Press, Minneapolis. © 1956 University of Minnesota: 133.

From *A System of Architectural Ornament* by Louis Sullivan, courtesy of the American Institute of Architects: 154.

INDEX

Page numbers in italic indicate illustrations.
The following abbreviations are used to indicate the architect associated with certain index entries

A&S: Adler & Sullivan   J&E: Johnston & Edelmann
B&R: Burnham & Root   R: Richardson
   F: Furness   S: Sullivan
   J: Jenney   W: Wright

acoustics, 81, 92, 161
Adler, Abraham, 125, 127
Adler, Dankmar, 67–70, 68, 72, 79–83, 85–89, 92, 94, 98, 101, 105–107, 113–114, 121, 124–128, 131, 139, 142
Adler, Dila, 107
Adler, Sidney, 125, 127
Administration Building (Chicago, World's Fair), 116
Algona, Iowa, S's bank in, 144
arches, 41, 83, 131, 161
Architectural League, 136
Art Institute of Chicago, 80
artificial loading, 88–89
Auditorium Building (Chicago, A&S), 82–83, 84, 85–89, 89–91, 92–94, 102
Autobiography of an Idea, The (Sullivan), 152–153, 155–156

banks, "strongbox," designed by S, 144, 146

Bayard Building (New York, S), 129, *130*, 131
Bessemer, Henry, 75
Borden Block (Chicago, A&S), 70, 71, 72, 77, 88, 105
Boston, Mass., 6–7, *19*, 20, 21, 37–38; S's impressions of, 17–18, 20–22
Brattle Square Church (Boston, R), 39, 40
Brimmer School (Boston), 18
Buffalo, N.Y.:
Guaranty Building (A&S), 121, 122–123, 124, 131
Larkin Building (W), *148*
Burling, Edward, 67–69
Burnham, Daniel, 113–116, *114*, 119, 134

Carson, Pirie, Scott & Company. *See* Schlesinger & Mayer department store.
cast iron, 75, 79, 161
Charnley, James, 96–98, 109

Chicago:
  S's parents move to, 24; fire
    (1871), 35, 53; S's impressions
    of, 51; growth after fire, 73;
    construction problems in, 75,
    77, 88–89; World's Columbian
    Exposition in, 113–116, 118,
    121; depression of 1893 and,
    121, 124
Chicago Club, 98, 146
"Chicago school" of architecture,
    102, 115, 120–121
Clark, Newcomb, 97–98
Cliff Dwellers Club, 146, 149, 152
Clopet, M. (S's teacher), 58–60
Columbus, Wis., S's bank in, 144
columns, 87, 161
continuous foundation, 75, 87–88
cornice, 129, 161
Court of Honor (Chicago, World's
    Fair), 116, 117, 118–119
Craftsman, The, 143
Crane Elevator Company, 126–127
cupola, 83, 161

depressions, financial: 1873, 48–50,
    64; 1893, 121, 124
Dunning, Max, 153, 155

Eastport, Maine, 17
École des Beaux Arts (Paris), 38–
    39, 41, 55, 57–58, 62–64
Edelmann, John, 54–55, 59, 64, 67,
    69–70, 78
Electricity Building (Chicago,
    World's Fair), 116
elevator, invention of, 102
English High School (Boston), 30–
    36
Evans House (Chicago, W), *148*

Faneuil Hall (Boston), 20
Festival Opera House (Chicago,
    A&S), 80–82, 92
fireproofing, 101
frescoes, 67, 162
Furness, Frank, 43–46, 47, 49–51,
    78

Golden Doorway, of Transportation
    Building (Chicago, World's
    Fair, A&S), 119, 120, 127
Gothic style, 78, 121, 162
Guarantee Trust and Safe Deposit
    Company (Phila., F), 47
Guaranty Building (Buffalo, A&S),
    121, *122–123,* 124, 131

Hale, Mr. (S's teacher), 35
Halifax, Nova Scotia, 17–18
Harrison, Benjamin, 92–93
Harvard University, 39
Hattabough, Margaret. *See* Sullivan,
    Margaret
Hewitt, George, 44–46, 49–50
Hewitt, John, 45
Home Insurance Building (Chicago,
    J), 75, 76, 103
Hunt, Richard Morris, 116, 118

*Interstate Architect and Builder,
    The,* 136
Interstate Exposition Building. *See*
    Festival Opera House

Jay Cooke & Company, 48
Jenney, William Le Baron, 51, 55,
    64, 67
Johnston, William, 64, 67
*Journal of the American Institute
    of Architects,* 152–153

Kindergarten Chats (Sullivan),
    136–137, 139, 152
Krause, William, 151
Krause Music Store (Chicago, S),
    151, *151*

Larkin Building (Buffalo, W), *148*
Latin School (Boston), 18, 30
Letang, Eugène, 38, 41, 62
List, Anna (S's grandmother), 3–4,
    6–9, 11
  illness and death, 33–34
List, Henri (S's grandfather), 3–4,
    4, 6–11, 33–34, 43, 48, 50
List, Julius (S's uncle), 43, 48
load-bearing walls, 87

London, S's visit to, 56
Lotus Place club, 54–55
Louisburg Square (Boston), 21

Machinery Hall (Chicago, World's Fair), 116
Marshall Field Wholesale Store (Chicago, R), 77–78, 82, 94, 95
masonry, 75–76, 79, 87, 94, 101–102, 162
Massachusetts Institute of Technology, 34–39, 37, 41
Mississippi River Levee Board, 109
Monadnock Building (Chicago, B&R), 74, 75, 113
Moody's Tabernacle (Chicago, J&E), 67
Morton, Levi P., 92–93
mullions, 131–132, 162

National Farmer's Bank, (Owatonna, Minn., S), 142–144, 144–145
New York City, 113, 142
Bayard Building, 129, 130, 131
Nimmons, George, 152, 155
Newburyport, Mass., 11, 13–14, 16
New Orleans:
S's visit to, 96; S's railroad station in, 109

Ocean Springs, Miss., S's home at, 96–98, 99, 109, 135, 137, 138, 139–140, 146, 153
Old North Church (Boston), 20
ornamentation, 41, 87, 92, 119, 121, 124, 132, 159, 162
Otis, Elisha G., 102
Owatonna, Minn., S's bank in, 142–144, 144–145

Paris, S's visit to, 57–63
Park Street Church (Boston), 20
Philadelphia, S's impression of, 43–44
piers, 77, 103, 104, 105, 121, 129, 131–132
Peck, Ferdinand, 80–83, 84–86, 93

Portland Block (Chicago, J), 51, 54
Provident Life and Trust Company Bank (Phila., F), 47
Pueblo, Colo., S's building in, 94

Republican National Convention (1888), 92
Rice Grammar School (Boston), 25–29
Richardson, Henry Hobson, 39, 40, 41, 46, 57–58, 64, 65, 77–78, 83, 94, 95, 116, 121
death, 82
Rogers Building (M.I.T.), 37
"Roman classic" style, 115–116, 117, 118
Romanesque style, 40, 41, 77, 121, 163
Root, John, 113–116, 115, 118

St. Louis, Mo., 113
Wainwright Building (A&S) 102–103, 104, 105, 121, 131
Salt Lake City, S's building in, 94
Schiller Building (Chicago, A&S), 105, 106
Schlesinger & Mayer department store (Chicago, S), 131–132, 133, 134, 136
setbacks, 105–106, 163
settlement, 88, 163
Sidney, Ohio, S's bank in, 144
Singer Building (New York), 142
skeleton construction, 75–76
South Reading, Mass., 6–7, 17–18
spandrels, 105, 121, 163
Spelman, Mr., 109–110
Spelman, Mary. See Sullivan, Mary
State House (Boston), 20, 20
steel, 75, 79, 101–102, 163
Sullivan, Albert (S's brother), 5, 6–7, 9, 18, 24, 35, 50–51, 54–55, 64, 79–80, 83, 93, 99, 109, 110; marriage, 110–111; estrangement from Louis, 112
Sullivan, Andrienne (S's mother), 5, 6–7, 11–13, 15, 18, 20, 24–25, 50, 79, 83, 99; death, 101

Sullivan, Louis:

birth, 6; relationship with father, 13–15; impressions of Boston, 17–18, 20–22; decides to become an architect, 23–24, 29; grandmother's death, 33–34; Richardson's influence upon, 41, 77–78, 82–83, 94; impressions of Philadelphia, 43–44; with Furness & Hewitt, 44–50; with Jenney, 51, 54–55; visits London, 56; stay in Paris, 57–63; with Johnston & Edelmann, 67; joins Adler, 70; enters partnership with Adler, 72; father's death, 79; meets Wright, 86–87; home in Ocean Springs, 96–98, *99*, 109, 135, 137, *138*, 139–140, 146, 153; mother's death, 101; reaction to Albert's marriage, 110–112; opinion of style at Columbian Exposition, 116, 118, 120–121; falling out with Wright, 124–125; Adler dissolves partnership, 126; drinking, 128, 139–140; marriage, 135–141; divorce, 141; last illness, 155–156; death, 158

EDUCATION: grade school, 7–11; at Brimmer School, 18; at Rice Grammar School, 25–29; at English High (Boston), 30–33, 35; at M.I.T., 36–42; at École des Beaux Arts, 57–63

THEORY OF ARCHITECTURE, 41, 54, 78–79, 113, 136–137, 143, 158

ILLUSTRATIONS OF, *frontis*, *5*, *27*, *66*, *97*, *108*

BUILDINGS: Borden Block, 70, *71*, *72*, 77, 88, 105; Festival Opera House, 80–82, *92*; Auditorium Building, 82–83, *84*, *85–89*, *89–91*, *92–94*, 102; Walker Warehouse, 94, *95;* mother's house, *100*, 101; Wainwright Building, 102–103, *104*, 105, 121, 131;

Schiller Building, 105, *106;* Transportation Building, 115, 118–119, *118*, 121, 127, 131, 144; Guaranty Building, 121, *122–123*, *124*, 131; Bayard Building, 129, *130*, 131; Schlesinger & Mayer dept. store, 131–132, *133*, *134*, 136; National Farmer's Bank, 142–144, *144–145;* "strongbox" banks, 144, 146; Krause Music Store, 151, *151*

WRITINGS, 143, 155: "Young Man in Architecture, The," 136; *Kindergarten Chats*, 136–137, 139, 152; *Autobiography of an Idea, The*, 152–153, 155–156; *System of Architectural Ornament*, 153, *154*, 155

Sullivan, Mary (S's sister-in-law), 110–112, *111*

Sullivan, Margaret (S's wife), 135–137, *138*, 139–141

Sullivan, Patrick (S's father), 5, 6–7, 13–18, 24–25, 50, 55, 63; death, 79–80

System of Architectural Ornament According with a Philosophy of Man's Powers, A, (Sullivan), 153, *154*, 155

Tacoma Building (Chicago), 103

terra-cotta, 104, 121, 122–23, 129, 132, 151

Tompson family, 34–35

Tompson, George, 28, 34–36, 41–42

Tower Building (New York), 103

Transportation Building (Chicago, World's Fair, A&S), 115, 118–119, *118*, 121, 127, 131, 144

Trinity Church (Boston, R), 64, 65

turrets, 83, 163

Wainwright, Ellis, 102

Wainwright Building (St. Louis, A&S), 102–103, *104*, 105, 121, 131

Wakefield, Cyrus, 18

Wakefield, Mass., 18

Walker Warehouse (Chicago, A&S), 94, 95

Ware, William, 38–39, 41, 62; opinion on the Auditorium Building, 85–86

Washington, D.C., 113

Wheelock, Mr. (headmaster, Rice Grammar School), 27–28

Woolson, Moses, 30–33, 35, 39, 58

Woolworth Building (New York), 142

World's Columbian Exposition (Chicago), 113–121, 117, 127

Wright, Frank Lloyd, 86–87, 103, 124–125, 129, 147, 147, 148, 149, 154–156, 158–159

Vaudremer, Emile, 62

"Young Man in Architecture, The" (Sullivan), 136

2016